Math Achievement
Enriching Activities Based on NCTM Standards

Grade 4

by
**Gina Monteleone
and Jennifer Moore**

Table of Contents

Introduction

Welcome to the **Math Achievement** series! Each book in this series is designed to reinforce the math skills appropriate for each grade level and to encourage high-level thinking and problem-solving skills. Enhancing students' thinking and problem-solving abilities can help them succeed in all academic areas. In addition, experiencing success in math can increase a student's confidence and self-esteem, both in and out of the classroom.

Each **Math Achievement** book offers challenging questions **based on the standards specified by the National Council of Teachers of Mathematics (NCTM)**. All five content standards (number and operations, algebra, geometry, measurement, data analysis and probability) and the process standard, problem solving, are covered in the activities.

The questions and format are similar to those found on standardized math tests. The experience students gain from answering questions in this format may help increase their test scores.

These exercises can be used to enhance the regular math curriculum, to individualize instruction, to provide extra practice for home schoolers, or to review skills between grades.

Each **Math Achievement** book contains **four pretests in standardized test format** at the beginning of each book. The pretests have been designed so that they may be used individually, as four stand-alone tests, or in groups. They may be used to identify students' needs in specific areas, or to compare students' math abilities at the beginning and end of the school year. **A scoring box is also included on each activity page**. This scoring box can be programmed to suit your specific classroom and student needs with total problems, total correct, and score.

The following math skills are covered in this book:

- **problem solving**
- **place value**
- **rounding**
- **estimation**
- **addition**
- **subtraction**
- **multiplication**
- **division**
- **fractions**
- **decimals**
- **calendar**
- **time**
- **money**
- **measurement**
- **geometry**
- **tables and graphs**

Name _____

Pretest

Read each problem. Then, circle the letter beside the correct answer.

1.
$$27 + 59$$

A. 78   C. 86
B. 72   D. 82

2.
$$394 + 246$$

A. 550   C. 630
B. 640   D. 540

3.
$$82 - 16$$

A. 66   C. 74
B. 64   D. 96

4.
$$531 - 162$$

A. 431   C. 331
B. 469   D. 369

5. $500 + 30 + 2 =$

A. 523
B. 325
C. 532
D. 235

6. $6{,}000 + 400 + 20 + 1 =$

A. 2,461
B. 2,164
C. 6,124
D. 6,421

7.   32 is closest to:

A. 30
B. 40
C. 20
D. 10

8.   179 is closest to:

A. 100
B. 700
C. 900
D. 200

9.
$$21 \times 5$$

A. 151   C. 125
B. 105   D. 115

10.
$$382 \times 3$$

A. 1,126   C. 946
B. 1,046   D. 1,146

11.
$$104 \times 32$$

A. 3,328   C. 3,108
B. 3,028   D. 2,012

12.
$$5{,}217 \times 24$$

A. 125,028   C. 125,208
B. 140,234   D. 152,452

13.   Joan read one book with 175 pages, one with 351 pages, and one with 539 pages. How many pages did she read in all?

A. 1,065   C. 710
B. 1,503   D. 1,042

14.   George worked a jigsaw puzzle with 1,500 pieces. Bob worked one with 750 pieces. How many more pieces did George's puzzle have?

A. 175   C. 750
B. 850   D. 749

4

Total Problems: _____   Total Correct: _____   Score: _____

© Carson-Dellosa CD-2211

Name _____

Read each problem. Then, circle the letter beside the correct answer.

1. The best estimate for 23 x 38 is _____.

   A. 20 x 30
   B. 30 x 40
   C. 20 x 40
   D. 30 x 30

2. The best estimate of the product of 67 x 22 is _____.

   A. 1,000
   B. 1,200
   C. 1,500
   D. 1,400

3. Alex bought paper plates for a party. There were 24 plates in each package, and she bought 12 packages. How many plates did she buy?

   A. 288   B. 360   C. 248   D. 240

4. In Julie's building, there are 135 apartments on 9 floors. There are the same number of apartments on each floor. How many apartments are on each floor?

   A. 19   B. 15   C. 25   D. 17

5. $12\overline{)96}$

   A. 7
   B. 8
   C. 6
   D. 9

6. $34\overline{)204}$

   A. 5
   B. 7
   C. 4
   D. 6

7. $5\overline{)38,675}$

   A. 7,735
   B. 8,111
   C. 9,103
   D. 7,525

8. $24\overline{)13,656}$

   A. 596
   B. 658
   C. 356
   D. 569

9. $21\overline{)4,893}$

   A. 233
   B. 223 R19
   C. 324
   D. 231 R15

10. $6\overline{)78,932}$

   A. 12,305
   B. 14,729
   C. 13,153 R2
   D. 13,155 R2

11. Mary needs index cards for her science project. She bought a pack of 200. If she shares them equally with 3 other people working on the project, how many will each person get?

   A. 66   B. 140   C. 71   D. 50

12. Andrew has 15 friends coming for his birthday party. His mom bought an assortment of chips that contains 36 bags. If Andrew and his friends each have 2 bags of chips, how many will be left over?

   A. 6   B. 3   C. 5   D. 4

Total Problems:	Total Correct:	Score:

Read each problem. Then, circle the letter beside the correct answer.

1. Which figure is symmetrical?

   A.   C.

   B.   D.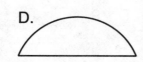

2. Which figures are congruent?

   A.    C.

   B.    D.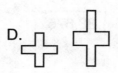

3. Which is a right angle?

   A.   C.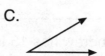

   B.    D.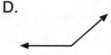

4. Which is an acute angle?

   A. 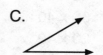   C.

   B. 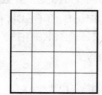   D.

5. What is the area of this figure?

   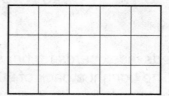

   A.   9 square units
   B.   16 square units
   C.   12 square units
   D.   20 square units

6. What is the perimeter of this figure?

   A.   16 units
   B.   15 units
   C.   18 units
   D.   25 units

Total Problems: _____   Total Correct: _____   Score: _____

Name _____   **Pretest**

Read each problem. Then, circle the letter beside the correct answer.

1. Which is the best unit for measuring a pencil?

    A. kilometer
    B. meter
    C. centimeter

2. What is the best unit for measuring the height of a flagpole?

    A. inch
    B. mile
    C. yard

3. What is the best unit for measuring liquid in a bucket?

    A. gallon
    B. pint
    C. ounce

4. What part of this figure is shaded?

    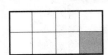

    A. $\frac{1}{4}$ B. $\frac{1}{2}$ C. $\frac{1}{3}$ D. $\frac{1}{8}$

5. Which figure shows $\frac{1}{3}$ shaded?

6. Which figure has the largest part shaded?

    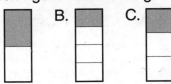

7. Which fraction represents the largest part of a figure?

    A. $\frac{1}{2}$ B. $\frac{1}{4}$ C. $\frac{1}{3}$

8. Which are equivalent fractions?

    A. $\frac{1}{2}$ and $\frac{2}{4}$ C. $\frac{1}{3}$ and $\frac{2}{3}$

    B. $\frac{1}{3}$ and $\frac{2}{4}$ D. $\frac{1}{2}$ and $\frac{1}{3}$

9. $\frac{1}{4} + \frac{1}{4} =$ _____

    A. $\frac{1}{2}$ B. 1   C. $\frac{2}{8}$ D. $\frac{1}{8}$

10. $\frac{1}{2} + \frac{1}{4} =$ _____

    A. $\frac{1}{6}$ B. $\frac{1}{4}$ C. $\frac{3}{4}$ D. $\frac{2}{6}$

11. Which shows $\frac{1}{10}$ written as a decimal?

    A. 0.3   B. 0.1   C. 0.5

12. Which shows $\frac{75}{100}$ written as a decimal?

    A. 0.75   B. 0.100   C. 7.5

Total Problems: _____   **Total Correct:** _____   **Score:** _____

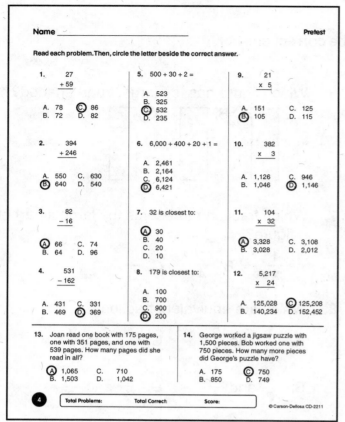

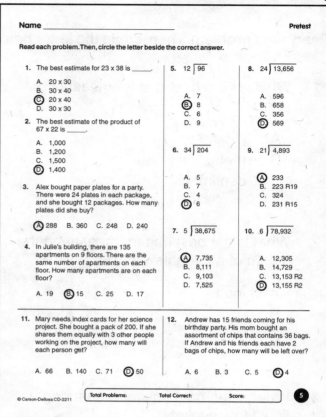

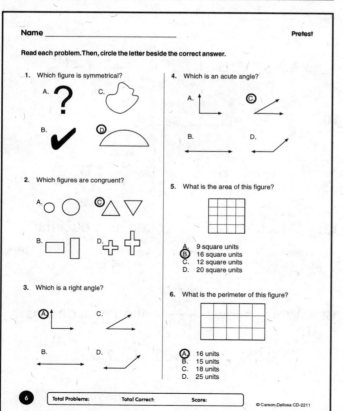

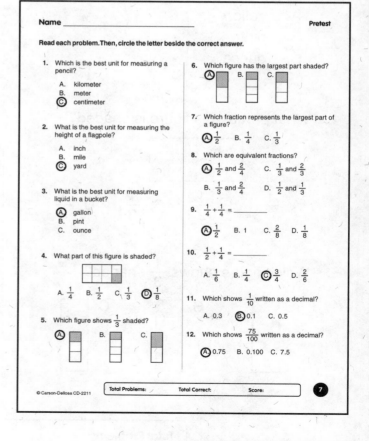

Top-left worksheet (page 4):

Name _____ Pretest

Read each problem. Then, circle the letter beside the correct answer.

1. 27
    + 59

    A. 78   (C.) 86
    B. 72   D. 82

2. 394
    + 246

    A. 550   C. 630
    (B.) 640   D. 540

3. 82
    − 16

    (A.) 66   C. 74
    B. 64   D. 96

4. 531
    − 162

    A. 431   C. 331
    B. 469   (D.) 369

5. 500 + 30 + 2 =

    A. 523
    B. 325
    (C.) 532
    D. 235

6. 6,000 + 400 + 20 + 1 =

    A. 2,461
    B. 2,164
    C. 6,124
    (D.) 6,421

7. 32 is closest to:

    (A.) 30
    B. 40
    C. 20
    D. 10

8. 179 is closest to:

    A. 100
    B. 700
    C. 900
    (D.) 200

9. 21
    x 5

    A. 151   C. 125
    (B.) 105   D. 115

10. 382
     x 3

    A. 1,126   C. 946
    B. 1,046   (D.) 1,146

11. 104
     x 32

    (A.) 3,328   C. 3,108
    B. 3,028   D. 2,012

12. 5,217
     x 24

    A. 125,028   (C.) 125,208
    B. 140,234   D. 152,452

13. Joan read one book with 175 pages, one with 351 pages, and one with 539 pages. How many pages did she read in all?

    (A.) 1,065   C. 710
    B. 1,503   D. 1,042

14. George worked a jigsaw puzzle with 1,500 pieces. Bob worked one with 750 pieces. How many more pieces did George's puzzle have?

    A. 175   (C.) 750
    B. 850   D. 749

Total Problems: ___ Total Correct: ___ Score: ___

4   © Carson-Dellosa CD-2211

Top-right worksheet (page 5):

Name _____ Pretest

Read each problem. Then, circle the letter beside the correct answer.

1. The best estimate for 23 x 38 is _____.

    A. 20 x 30
    B. 30 x 40
    (C.) 20 x 40
    D. 30 x 30

2. The best estimate of the product of 67 x 22 is _____.

    A. 1,000
    B. 1,200
    C. 1,500
    (D.) 1,400

3. Alex bought paper plates for a party. There were 24 plates in each package, and she bought 12 packages. How many plates did she buy?

    (A.) 288   B. 360   C. 248   D. 240

4. In Julie's building, there are 135 apartments on 9 floors. There are the same number of apartments on each floor. How many apartments are on each floor?

    A. 19   (B.) 15   C. 25   D. 17

5. 12 ⟌ 96

    A. 7
    (B.) 8
    C. 6
    D. 9

6. 34 ⟌ 204

    A. 5
    B. 7
    C. 4
    (D.) 6

7. 5 ⟌ 38,675

    (A.) 7,735
    B. 8,111
    C. 9,103
    D. 7,525

8. 24 ⟌ 13,656

    A. 596
    B. 658
    C. 356
    (D.) 569

9. 21 ⟌ 4,893

    (A.) 233
    B. 223 R19
    C. 324
    D. 231 R15

10. 6 ⟌ 78,932

    A. 12,305
    B. 14,729
    C. 13,153 R2
    (D.) 13,155 R2

11. Mary needs index cards for her science project. She bought a pack of 200. If she shares them equally with 3 other people working on the project, how many will each person get?

    A. 66   B. 140   C. 71   (D.) 50

12. Andrew has 15 friends coming for his birthday party. His mom bought an assortment of chips that contains 36 bags. If Andrew and his friends each have 2 bags of chips, how many will be left over?

    A. 6   B. 3   C. 5   (D.) 4

Total Problems: ___ Total Correct: ___ Score: ___

© Carson-Dellosa CD-2211   5

Bottom-left worksheet (page 6):

Name _____ Pretest

Read each problem. Then, circle the letter beside the correct answer.

1. Which figure is symmetrical?

2. Which figures are congruent?

3. Which is a right angle?

4. Which is an acute angle?

5. What is the area of this figure?

    A. 9 square units
    (B.) 16 square units
    C. 12 square units
    D. 20 square units

6. What is the perimeter of this figure?

    (A.) 16 units
    B. 15 units
    C. 18 units
    D. 25 units

Total Problems: ___ Total Correct: ___ Score: ___

6   © Carson-Dellosa CD-2211

Bottom-right worksheet (page 7):

Name _____ Pretest

Read each problem. Then, circle the letter beside the correct answer.

1. Which is the best unit for measuring a pencil?

    A. kilometer
    B. meter
    (C.) centimeter

2. What is the best unit for measuring the height of a flagpole?

    A. inch
    B. mile
    (C.) yard

3. What is the best unit for measuring liquid in a bucket?

    (A.) gallon
    B. pint
    C. ounce

4. What part of this figure is shaded?

    A. $\frac{1}{4}$ B. $\frac{1}{2}$ C. $\frac{1}{3}$ (D.) $\frac{1}{8}$

5. Which figure shows $\frac{1}{3}$ shaded?

6. Which figure has the largest part shaded?

7. Which fraction represents the largest part of a figure?

    (A.) $\frac{1}{2}$ B. $\frac{1}{4}$ C. $\frac{1}{3}$

8. Which are equivalent fractions?

    (A.) $\frac{1}{2}$ and $\frac{2}{4}$ C. $\frac{1}{3}$ and $\frac{2}{3}$
    B. $\frac{1}{3}$ and $\frac{2}{4}$ D. $\frac{1}{2}$ and $\frac{1}{3}$

9. $\frac{1}{4} + \frac{1}{4} =$ _____

    (A.) $\frac{1}{2}$ B. 1   C. $\frac{2}{8}$ D. $\frac{1}{8}$

10. $\frac{1}{2} + \frac{1}{4} =$ _____

    A. $\frac{1}{6}$ B. $\frac{1}{4}$ (C.) $\frac{3}{4}$ D. $\frac{2}{6}$

11. Which shows $\frac{1}{10}$ written as a decimal?

    A. 0.3   (B.) 0.1   C. 0.5

12. Which shows $\frac{75}{100}$ written as a decimal?

    (A.) 0.75   B. 0.100   C. 7.5

Total Problems: ___ Total Correct: ___ Score: ___

© Carson-Dellosa CD-2211   7

8

Study the example below. Write the value of each underlined digit on the line provided.

Example:

	Millions			Thousands			Ones		
Hundred Millions	Ten Millions	Millions	Hundred Thousands	Ten Thousands	Thousands	Hundreds	Tens	Ones
5	0	3 ,	6	7	3 ,	<u>9</u>	8	2

The underlined digit **9** is in the hundreds place; therefore, it has a value of **900**.

1. 4<u>7</u>3

_____

2. 2,07<u>5</u>

_____

3. 2<u>8</u>,365

_____

4. 8<u>3</u>0,724

_____

5. <u>1</u>15,307

_____

6. <u>4</u>,781,326

_____

7. <u>9</u>4,320,188

_____

8. 1<u>3</u>3,278,245

_____

9. 64<u>9</u>,228,713

_____

10. <u>1</u>47,306,254

_____

11. <u>4</u>6,598

_____

12. <u>3</u>74,129

_____

13. <u>2</u>57,123,448

_____

14. 73<u>2</u>,146,209

_____

Total Problems: _____   Total Correct: _____   Score: _____

Study the box below. Then, write each number in standard numerical form on the line provided.

Rule:	Examples:
A number is usually written using digits in the appropriate place value spots. This is called standard form.	five thousand, two hundred fifty-one = **5,251** twenty-two thousand, thirty-three = **22,033**

1. seventeen thousand, four hundred thirty-three =

   _____

2. five thousand, eight hundred ninety-one =

   _____

3. six thousand, twenty-five =

   _____

4. three hundred forty-two thousand, six hundred eight =

   _____

5. seven hundred twenty-one thousand, nine hundred four =

   _____

6. one million, eight hundred twenty thousand, five hundred fifteen =

   _____

7. one hundred million, forty-three thousand, sixteen =

   _____

8. seventy-one million, eight hundred forty-one thousand, five hundred four =

   _____

9. nine billion, eighty-three million, six hundred two thousand, five hundred =

   _____

10. sixty-five million, eight hundred forty thousand, three =

    _____

11. sixty-one thousand, eight =

    _____

12. ninety-five billion, eight hundred seventy-three million, two hundred thousand, five hundred ninety-two =

    _____

Total Problems:	Total Correct:	Score:

Name _____

Study the examples below. Then, circle the letter beside the correct answer.

Examples:

$3,000 + 100 + 20 + 8 = \mathbf{3,128}$
$800,000 + 10,000 + 30 + 2 = \mathbf{810,032}$

1. $5,000 + 300 + 20 + 8 =$
   A. 50,328
   B. 5,328
   C. 538
   D. 503,208

2. $800 + 30 + 6 =$
   A. 8,036
   B. 8,306
   C. 836
   D. 386

3. $20,000 + 3,000 + 200 + 8 =$
   A. 2,328
   B. 23,280
   C. 20,208
   D. 23,208

4. $80,000 + 1,000 + 50 + 6 =$
   A. 81,056
   B. 8,560
   C. 8,156
   D. 80,506

5. $700,000 + 20,000 + 2,000, + 100 + 70 =$
   A. 722,170
   B. 702,170
   C. 72,217
   D. 7,217

6. $4,000,000 + 800,000 + 60,000 + 20 =$
   A. 4,086,020
   B. 4,860,020
   C. 486,020
   D. 408,620

7. $9,000,000 + 70,000 + 300 + 80 + 6 =$
   A. 970,386
   B. 9,070,386
   C. 907,386
   D. 973,086

8. $50,000 + 6,000 + 800 + 90 =$
   A. 56,890
   B. 5,689
   C. 50,689
   D. 56,809

Total Problems: **Total Correct:**   **Score:**

Study the box below. Round each number to 10, then 100. Then, write the answer on the line provided.

Rules:	Examples:
Round numbers to the nearest 10 by checking the digit in the ones place value spot. If that digit is 5 or greater, round up to the next 10. If it is 4 or lower, keep the same 10.	9,483 = Nearest 10: **9,480** Nearest 100: **9,500**
Round numbers to the nearest 100 by checking the digit in the tens place value spot. If that digit is 5 or greater, round up to the next 10. If it is 4 or lower, keep the same 100.	2,795 = Nearest 10: **2,800** Nearest 100: **2,800**

1. 422

    Nearest 10 _____

    Nearest 100 _____

2. 338

    Nearest 10 _____

    Nearest 100 _____

3. 659

    Nearest 10 _____

    Nearest 100 _____

4. 785

    Nearest 10 _____

    Nearest 100 _____

5. 984

    Nearest 10 _____

    Nearest 100 _____

6. 1,342

    Nearest 10 _____

    Nearest 100 _____

7. 1,758

    Nearest 10 _____

    Nearest 100 _____

8. 24,317

    Nearest 10 _____

    Nearest 100 _____

9. 65,284

    Nearest 10 _____

    Nearest 100 _____

10. 248,739

    Nearest 10 _____

    Nearest 100 _____

11. 462,145

    Nearest 10 _____

    Nearest 100 _____

12. 3,241,458

    Nearest 10 _____

    Nearest 100 _____

13. 569,347

    Nearest 10 _____

    Nearest 100 _____

14. 3,760,199

    Nearest 10 _____

    Nearest 100 _____

15. 7,789,984

    Nearest 10 _____

    Nearest 100 _____

Total Problems: **Total Correct:**   **Score:**

Round to the nearest thousand. Then, write the answer on the line provided.

1. 5,384 _____

2. 7,521 _____

3. 8,432 _____

4. 62,381 _____

5. 76,432 _____

6. 82,197 _____

7. 94,306 _____

8. 738,149 _____

Round to the nearest million. Then, write the answer on the line provided.

9. 2,438,692 _____

10. 6,743,214 _____

11. 84,329,167 _____

12. 98,724,410 _____

13. 60,213,548 _____

14. 106,247,596 _____

15. 851,463,462 _____

16. 99,543,873 _____

Round to the nearest billion. Then, write the answer on the line provided.

17. 5,432,687,155 _____

18. 7,541,320,152 _____

19. 14,362,188,206 _____

20. 37,548,139,664 _____

21. 74,324,145,306 _____

22. 75,334,509,438 _____

23. 146,788,129,365 _____

24. 248,175,379,912 _____

25. 598,375,287,032 _____

26. 129,644,321,014 _____

Total Problems:	Total Correct:	Score:

Name _____

Solve each word problem. Then, write the answer in the space provided.

1. Write the number:

    Seven tens, five hundreds, six ones, seven thousands

2. Write the number:

    Five thousand larger than twenty-five thousand

3. Write the number:

    Eighty thousand larger than four hundred twelve

4. Write the number:

    Seven million less than twenty-one million, eight hundred forty-three thousand, six

5. Write the larger number, using numerals.

    A. Sixty-four thousand, two hundred

    B. Four hundred three thousand, twelve

6. Sam and Joseph went to the championship football game and saw twenty-eight thousand people. Write the number using numerals.

7. Bobby and Janet flew 2,854 miles to their grandparents' house. Their cousins' flight was 13,492 miles. Who had farther to fly?

8. A company spent eight billion, eight million, ninety-five thousand dollars in one year for their employees. Write this number using numerals.

14

| Total Problems: | Total Correct: | Score: |

Add. Then, write the sum on the line provided.

1. 4 + 8 = _____

2. 7 + 5 = _____

3. 9 + 9 = _____

4. 6 + 7 = _____

5. 8 + 3 = _____

6. 4 + 6 = _____

7. 5 + 9 = _____

8. 7 + 8 = _____

9. 5 + 8 = _____

10. 7 + 7 = _____

11. 9 + 2 = _____

12. 10 + 11 = _____

13. (4 + 2) + (8 + 1) = _____

14. 9 + (3 + 6) = _____

15. 9 + 7 + 3 = _____

16. 5 + (4 + 9) + 2 = _____

17. (8 + 6) + 3 = _____

18. (9 + 5) + (3 + 8) = _____

19. (7 + 1) + (8 + 8) = _____

20. 4 + 2 + 6 = _____

21. (3 + 3) + (8 + 9) = _____

22. (5 + 4) + (2 + 4) + 6 = _____

23. (7 + 9) + (5 + 5) = _____

24. (4 + 6) + (2 + 9) = _____

Total Problems: Total Correct: Score:

Name _____

Study the examples below. Use the comparison symbols >, <, or = to complete the number sentences below. Then, place the symbol in the square provided.

Examples:

2 + 3 **<** 1 + 5 | 6 + 1 **>** 4 + 2 | (6 + 2) + 4 **=** (2 + 5) + 5

1. 3 + 8 ☐ 5 + 9

2. 6 + 7 ☐ 8 + 4

3. (3 + 9) + 5 ☐ 7 + 14

4. (3 + 6) + 2 ☐ (8 + 7) + 5

5. 6 + 4 ☐ 5 + 5

6. (8 + 2) + 6 ☐ (6 + 2) + 8

7. (5 + 2) + 9 ☐ (3 + 7)

8. (2 + 9) ☐ (3 + 7) + 7

9. 8 + (5 + 2) ☐ 7 + (8 + 3)

10. 4 + (3 + 8) ☐ 2 + (5 + 9)

11. (8 + 9) + 5 ☐ 5 + (9 + 6)

12. (4 + 10) + 8 ☐ (9 + 9) + 9

13. (3 + 7) + 7 ☐ (5 + 4) + 9

14. (11 + 3) + 8 ☐ 5 + (9 + 10)

16

Total Problems: _____ Total Correct: _____ Score: _____

Name _____

Study the box below. Then, add and write the answer in the space provided.

Rule:

1. Add the ones column, then regroup.

2. Add the tens column, then regroup.

3. Add the hundreds column, then regroup.

4. Continue to add columns and regroup as needed.

Example:

$$
\begin{array}{r} {}^{1} \\ 217,388 \\ +\,692,438 \\ \hline 6 \end{array}
\quad
\begin{array}{r} {}^{11} \\ 217,388 \\ +\,692,438 \\ \hline 26 \end{array}
\quad
\begin{array}{r} {}^{11} \\ 217,388 \\ +\,692,438 \\ \hline 826 \end{array}
\quad
\begin{array}{r} {}^{11} \\ 217,388 \\ +\,692,438 \\ \hline 9,826 \end{array}
\quad
\begin{array}{r} {}^{1\;11} \\ 217,388 \\ +\,692,438 \\ \hline 09,826 \end{array}
\quad
\begin{array}{r} {}^{1\;11} \\ 217,388 \\ +\,692,438 \\ \hline \mathbf{909,826} \end{array}
$$

1. 15 + 6

2. 24 + 17

3. 18 + 13

4. 25 + 15

5. 48 + 29

6. 37 + 27

7. 59 + 26

8. 63 + 38

9. 65 + 39

10. 95 + 67

11. 73 + 58

12. 99 + 25

13. 112 + 48

14. 123 + 59

15. 238 + 76

16. 264 + 87

Total Problems: _____ Total Correct: _____ Score: _____

Add. Then, write the answer in the space provided.

1. 543
    + 27

2. 684
    + 175

3. 7,543
    + 287

4. 9,492
    + 1,368

5. 351
    + 347

6. 3,764
    + 2,883

7. 3,429
    + 8,462

8. 76,182
    + 34,245

9. 80,996
    + 36,215

10. 23,648
    + 41,295

11. 43,204
    + 23,524

12. 68,242
    + 35,254

13. 173,249
    + 56,245

14. 324,159
    + 278,634

15. 543,286
    + 215,740

16. 49,320
    + 36,249

17. 624,193
    + 453,126

18. 753,091
    + 773,256

19. 785,122
    + 542,137

20. 85,911
    + 28,347

18

Total Problems: Total Correct: Score:

Name _____

Study the examples below. Round each addend to the greatest place value. Then, add and write the answer in the space provided.

Examples:

59	rounds to	60		476	rounds to	500
+ 32	rounds to	+ 30		+ 35	rounds to	+ 40
		90				**540**

1. 46
    + 32

2. 56
    + 75

3. 88
    + 62

4. 125
    + 73

5. 236
    + 88

6. 565
    + 217

7. 609
    + 233

8. 1,753
    + 258

9. 13,954
    + 5,268

10. 25,694
    + 15,507

11. 136,284
    + 98,509

12. 248,139
    + 176,905

13. 603,897
    + 562,533

14. 375,218
    + 188,273

15. 492,376
    + 99,495

Total Problems: **Total Correct:**   **Score:**

Name _____

Solve each word problem. Show your work. Then, write the answer in the space provided.

---

1. Jason has 14 baseball cards in his collection. He buys 12 more. How many cards does Jason have now?

4. Natalie practiced her violin for 3 hours on Thursday, 2 hours on Friday, and 1 hour on both Saturday and Sunday. How many hours did she practice in all?

---

2. Stephanie walked 4 miles on Monday, 6 miles on Tuesday, and 7 miles on Wednesday for her school walk-a-thon. How many miles did she walk in all?

5. Devon drove his new sports car 45 miles the first day, 72 miles the second day, and 31 miles the third day. How many miles did he drive his sports car in all?

---

3. Scott played video games for 5 hours on Saturday. On Sunday, he played 4 hours longer than he did on Saturday. How many hours did Scott play video games in all?

6. The theater sold 462 tickets for the 4:00 P.M. show and 362 tickets for the 7:00 P.M. show. How many tickets were sold in all?

20

| Total Problems: | Total Correct: | Score: |

Name _____

Subtract. Write the answer on the line provided.

1. 9 − 5 = _____

2. 8 − 3 = _____

3. 7 − 2 = _____

4. 10 − 6 = _____

5. 12 − 6 = _____

6. 6 − 4 = _____

7. 8 − 6 = _____

8. 9 − 6 = _____

9. 11 − 6 = _____

10. 13 − 7 = _____

11. 15 − 9 = _____

12. 18 − 5 = _____

13. (8 − 3) − 1 = _____

14. (6 − 2) − 4 = _____

15. 9 − (18 − 13) = _____

16. (9 − 5) − (6 − 4) = _____

17. (12 − 5) − (8 − 3) = _____

18. (15 − 4) − (13 − 9) = _____

19. (16 − 8) − (9 − 4) = _____

20. (20 − 10) − (8 − 7) = _____

21. (40 − 10) − (30 − 15) = _____

22. (25 − 15) − (10 − 5) = _____

23. (18 − 5) − (16 − 10) = _____

24. (28 − 10) − (15 − 5) = _____

Total Problems:	Total Correct:	Score:

Study the box below. Subtract. Then, write the answer in the space provided.

Rule:

1. Regroup, then subtract the ones column.

2. Regroup, then subtract the tens column.

3. Regroup, then subract the hundreds column.

4. Continue to subtract columns and regroup as needed.

   When you regroup, the number to the left is decreased by one.

Example:

$$
\begin{array}{r} ^{2\,15}\ 342{,}5\cancel{3}5 \\ -\ 147{,}079 \\ \hline 6 \end{array}
\qquad
\begin{array}{r} ^{4\,12\,15}\ 342{,}\cancel{5}35 \\ -\ 147{,}079 \\ \hline 56 \end{array}
\qquad
\begin{array}{r} ^{4\,12\,15}\ 342{,}535 \\ -\ 147{,}079 \\ \hline 456 \end{array}
\qquad
\begin{array}{r} ^{3\,12\ \ 4\,12\,15}\ 34\cancel{2}{,}535 \\ -\ 147{,}079 \\ \hline 5{,}456 \end{array}
\qquad
\begin{array}{r} ^{2\,13\,12\,4\ \,12\,15}\ \cancel{3}42{,}535 \\ -\ 147{,}079 \\ \hline 95{,}456 \end{array}
\qquad
\begin{array}{r} ^{2\,13\,12\,4\ \,12\,15}\ 342{,}535 \\ -\ 147{,}079 \\ \hline \mathbf{195{,}456} \end{array}
$$

1. $\begin{array}{r}15 \\ -\ 8 \\ \hline \end{array}$	**5.** $\begin{array}{r}125 \\ -\ 78 \\ \hline \end{array}$	**9.** $\begin{array}{r}6{,}562 \\ -\ 688 \\ \hline \end{array}$	**13.** $\begin{array}{r}45{,}162 \\ -\ 29{,}798 \\ \hline \end{array}$
2. $\begin{array}{r}53 \\ -\ 19 \\ \hline \end{array}$	**6.** $\begin{array}{r}139 \\ -\ 64 \\ \hline \end{array}$	**10.** $\begin{array}{r}7{,}541 \\ -\ 2{,}975 \\ \hline \end{array}$	**14.** $\begin{array}{r}75{,}334 \\ -\ 28{,}567 \\ \hline \end{array}$
3. $\begin{array}{r}62 \\ -\ 47 \\ \hline \end{array}$	**7.** $\begin{array}{r}465 \\ -\ 298 \\ \hline \end{array}$	**11.** $\begin{array}{r}12{,}133 \\ -\ 9{,}742 \\ \hline \end{array}$	**15.** $\begin{array}{r}85{,}665 \\ -\ 38{,}777 \\ \hline \end{array}$
4. $\begin{array}{r}55 \\ -\ 37 \\ \hline \end{array}$	**8.** $\begin{array}{r}3{,}403 \\ -\ 597 \\ \hline \end{array}$	**12.** $\begin{array}{r}10{,}374 \\ -\ 8{,}585 \\ \hline \end{array}$	**16.** $\begin{array}{r}98{,}043 \\ -\ 75{,}968 \\ \hline \end{array}$

Total Problems: _____   **Total Correct:** _____   **Score:** _____

Name _____ **Subtracting Large Numbers**

Subtract. Then, write the answer in the space provided.

1. 2,375
  − 1,194

2. 6,000
  − 1,597

3. 2,758
  − 1,392

4. 7,594
  − 3,283

5. 62,913
  − 41,378

6. 413,206
  − 78,598

7. 375,211
  − 188,456

8. 754,326
  − 561,268

9. 743,245
  − 368,195

10. 954,328
  − 864,597

11. 880,372
  − 751,684

12. 3,298,174
  − 1,367,125

13. 4,369,211
  − 2,149,757

14. 7,354,147
  − 5,565,402

15. 9,507,366
  − 8,237,985

Total Problems: **Total Correct:**   **Score:**

Study the examples below. Round the minuend and subtrahend to the greatest place value. Then, subtract and write the answer in the space provided.

Examples:

576	rounds to	600		476	rounds to	500
− 328	rounds to	− 300		− 123	rounds to	− 100
		300				**400**

1.　　87
　　− 43

2.　　75
　　− 46

3.　　38
　　− 19

4.　　135
　　− 78

5.　　264
　　− 127

6.　　351
　　− 175

7.　　4,286
　　− 2,599

8.　　7,582
　　− 4,378

9.　　9,828
　　− 6,743

10.　　12,622
　　− 9,840

11.　　17,568
　　− 8,744

12.　　14,727
　　− 9,864

13.　　75,382
　　− 49,675

14.　　95,460
　　− 74,328

15.　　106,274
　　− 38,591

16.　　116,754
　　− 95,287

17.　　97,462
　　− 26,561

18.　　174,382
　　− 142,949

24

Total Problems:	Total Correct:	Score:

Name _____

Solve each problem. Show your work and write the answer in the space provided.

1. John had 23 baseball cards. He gave 11 to his friend at school. How many cards does John have left?

5. Jacob and Dominic collected 245 cans for the school can drive. They gave 55 cans to Dominic's little sister for her class to get credit. How many cans does this leave for the boys' class?

2. Mr. Faraday's farm has 285 cows. Of the 285, 115 of them are dairy cows. How many of Mr. Faraday's cows are not dairy cows?

6. Mr. Nelson had 346 boxes of merchandise to open and place on shelves at his store. In one day he emptied 284 boxes. How many boxes does he have left to open?

3. Molly stenciled 96 leaves on the art room's mural. Her teacher decided to cut the mural and remove 29 of the leaves Molly stenciled. How many leaves remain on the mural?

7. Dan bought 583 square yards of carpet for his basement. He only used 485 square yards. How much carpet did he have left?

4. Mr. Jackson bought 755 new golf tees. After one month of playing golf, he had lost or broken 294 of them. How many usable golf tees does he have left?

8. Selena has 114 compact discs of music in her collection. If she decides to give away 37 of them, how many will she have left?

Total Problems: _____ Total Correct: _____ Score: _____

Multiply. Write the answer on the line provided.

1. 9 x 6 = _____

2. 7 x 8 = _____

3. 6 x 7 = _____

4. 3 x 8 = _____

5. 3 x 5 = _____

6. 5 x 12 = _____

7. 3 x 4 = _____

8. 8 x 10 = _____

9. 9 x 2 = _____

10. 5 x 4 = _____

11. 4 x 7 = _____

12. 7 x 5 = _____

13. 5 x 5 = _____

14. 2 x 3 = _____

15. 6 x 3 = _____

16. 4 x 4 = _____

17. 8 x 5 = _____

18. 6 x 4 = _____

19. 6 x 5 = _____

20. 3 x 7 = _____

21. 4 x 8 = _____

22. 12 x 6 = _____

23. 7 x 7 = _____

24. 12 x 9 = _____

25. 9 x 5 = _____

26. 7 x 9 = _____

27. 12 x 5 = _____

28. 8 x 2 = _____

29. 5 x 2 = _____

30. 8 x 8 = _____

31. 6 x 6 = _____

32. 7 x 10 = _____

26

Total Problems: **Total Correct:**   **Score:**

Study the example below. Find the missing number and write the answer on the line provided.

> **Example:**
> (6 x _____) x 2 = 4 x 3   4 x 3 = 12, so (6 x _____) x 2 = 12
> (6 x __1__) x 2 = 4 x 3

1. _____ x 4 = 20

2. 7 x _____ = 49

3. _____ x 9 = 81

4. _____ x 7 = 42

5. _____ x 4 = 12

6. _____ x 6 = 36

7. _____ x 7 = 56

8. 9 x _____ = 27

9. 4 x _____ = 32

10. (5 x 2) x 3 = _____

11. (2 x 2) x 6 = _____

12. (7 x 4) x 1 = _____

13. (2 x 0) x 6 = _____

14. (3 x 3) x 5 = _____

15. (5 x 5) x 0 = _____

16. (5 x 9) x 2 = _____

17. (4 x 2) x 4 = _____

18. (6 x 3) x (5 x 2) = _____

19. (3 x 3) x (8 x 4) = _____

20. (7 x 4) x (9 x 3) = _____

21. (5 x _____) x 2 = 6 x 5

22. (2 x 10) x (5 x 1) = _____

23. (4 x 4) x 1 = 8 x _____

24. (_____ x 4) x 3 = 6 x 4

Total Problems: ___   Total Correct: ___   Score: ___

Name _____

Multiply. Then, write the answer in the space provided.

1.   10
  x 5

2.   20
  x 4

3.   60
  x 8

4.   90
  x 2

5.   50
  x 5

6.   40
  x 3

7.   80
  x 5

8.   30
  x 7

9.   30
  x 12

10.   50
  x 25

11. 200
  x 40

12. 800
  x 50

13. 500
  x 30

14. 700
  x 20

15. 400
  x 22

16. 900
  x 60

17. 8,000
  x   7

18. 6,000
  x   4

19. 5,000
  x 200

20. 3,000
  x 600

Total Problems: **Total Correct:**   **Score:**

Name _____

Multiply. Write the answer in the space provided.

1. 352
    x   28

5. 863
    x   74

9. 2,368
    x   127

13. 2,206
     x   700

2. 525
    x   64

6. 909
    x   83

10. 4,987
     x   521

14. 6,843
     x   811

3. 791
    x   37

7. 1,042
    x   68

11. 3,647
     x   86

15. 5,206
     x 1,673

4. 644
    x   92

8. 1,837
    x   55

12. 8,172
     x   348

16. 4,137
     x 3,275

Total Problems: Total Correct: Score:

Solve each word problem. Show your work and write the answer in the space provided.

1. Melanie bought 7 packages of greeting cards. Each package had 9 cards inside. How many greeting cards did she get in all?

5. Mr. Harding gave out 15 coupons per hour at the appliance show. After 2 days at the show, working 14 hours total, how many coupons did he distribute?

2. Grace saw 16 cages of birds at the zoo's aviary. The sign said each cage had 12 birds. How many birds were in the aviary cages in all?

6. Chris walked 4 miles a day for 21 days. How many miles did she walk in all?

3. Matthew unpacked 43 boxes of lightbulbs for the discount warehouse. Each box contained 6 bulbs. How many bulbs were there in all 43 boxes?

7. Kelly practiced her flute 30 minutes a day for 15 days. After the 15 days were completed, how many minutes had she practiced?

4. Nell sold 125 packages of cookies at the bake sale. Each package was tied with 2 ribbons. How many ribbons were used in all?

8. LaToya played her new CD for 3 hours every day the first 5 days she had it. How many hours did she play the CD? How many minutes was this?

34

Total Problems:	Total Correct:	Score:

Name _____

Divide. Write the answer on the line provided.

1. 9 ÷ 3 = _____

2. 24 ÷ 4 = _____

3. 49 ÷ 7 = _____

4. 32 ÷ 8 = _____

5. 25 ÷ 5 = _____

6. 16 ÷ 8 = _____

7. 35 ÷ 7 = _____

8. 20 ÷ 5 = _____

9. 12 ÷ 4 = _____

10. 15 ÷ 3 = _____

11. 24 ÷ 3 = _____

12. 36 ÷ 6 = _____

13. 60 ÷ 5 = _____

14. 18 ÷ 6 = _____

15. 80 ÷ 8 = _____

16. 18 ÷ 2 = _____

17. 40 ÷ 8 = _____

18. 108 ÷ 9 = _____

19. 30 ÷ 6 = _____

20. 45 ÷ 9 = _____

21. 42 ÷ 6 = _____

22. 28 ÷ 7 = _____

23. 63 ÷ 7 = _____

24. 90 ÷ 9 = _____

25. 56 ÷ 8 = _____

26. 21 ÷ 7 = _____

27. 16 ÷ 8 = _____

28. 6 ÷ 0 = _____

29. 54 ÷ 6 = _____

30. 64 ÷ 8 = _____

31. 10 ÷ 2 = _____

32. 21 ÷ 3 = _____

Total Problems: **Total Correct:** **Score:**

Study the box below. Divide and write the quotient in the space provided.

Rules:	Examples:
When a number is divided by 1, the quotient is the same as the number.	$1\overline{)5} = 5$ $0\overline{)15} = 0$
When a number is divided by 0, the quotient is 0.	

1. $1\overline{)7}$

2. $0\overline{)6}$

3. $1\overline{)8}$

4. $1\overline{)9}$

5. $1\overline{)3}$

6. $0\overline{)5}$

7. $0\overline{)2}$

8. $1\overline{)4}$

9. $1\overline{)2}$

10. $1\overline{)13}$

11. $0\overline{)25}$

12. $1\overline{)17}$

13. $1\overline{)12}$

14. $1\overline{)47}$

15. $0\overline{)28}$

16. $0\overline{)20}$

17. $1\overline{)79}$

18. $1\overline{)84}$

19. $0\overline{)76}$

20. $0\overline{)96}$

Total Problems: Total Correct: Score:

Study the box below. Divide and write the quotient in the space provided.

Rule:	Example:
Division is the opposite operation of multiplication.	$\begin{array}{r} 4 \\ \times\ 8 \\ \hline 32 \end{array}$ → $\begin{array}{r} 4 \\ 8\overline{)32} \end{array}$

1. $8\overline{)72}$

2. $9\overline{)63}$

3. $8\overline{)88}$

4. $8\overline{)64}$

5. $9\overline{)36}$

6. $8\overline{)40}$

7. $9\overline{)18}$

8. $8\overline{)16}$

9. $9\overline{)54}$

10. $9\overline{)45}$

11. $8\overline{)24}$

12. $8\overline{)240}$

13. $9\overline{)108}$

14. $8\overline{)816}$

15. $9\overline{)189}$

16. $8\overline{)320}$

17. $9\overline{)999}$

18. $9\overline{)819}$

19. $8\overline{)168}$

20. $8\overline{)408}$

Total Problems:　　**Total Correct:**　　**Score:**

Study the examples below. Divide and write the answer in the space provided.

Examples:

$$\begin{array}{r} 15 \\ 22\overline{)330} \\ -22 \\ \hline 110 \\ -110 \\ \hline 0 \end{array} \qquad \begin{array}{r} 23 \\ 41\overline{)943} \\ -82 \\ \hline 123 \\ -123 \\ \hline 0 \end{array}$$

1. $13\overline{)338}$ 5. $13\overline{)559}$ 9. $16\overline{)1,152}$ 13. $48\overline{)3,792}$

2. $24\overline{)432}$ 6. $46\overline{)690}$ 10. $29\overline{)3,567}$ 14. $27\overline{)2,376}$

3. $10\overline{)280}$ 7. $35\overline{)665}$ 11. $24\overline{)2,136}$ 15. $19\overline{)1,254}$

4. $16\overline{)320}$ 8. $18\overline{)828}$ 12. $17\overline{)1,071}$ 16. $52\overline{)4,108}$

38

Total Problems:	Total Correct:	Score:

Name _____   **Division with Five-Digit Dividends**

Divide, then write the answer in the space provided.

1. $46\overline{)19{,}550}$

4. $32\overline{)75{,}040}$

7. $84\overline{)19{,}824}$

10. $24\overline{)27{,}624}$

2. $71\overline{)24{,}850}$

5. $56\overline{)23{,}520}$

8. $62\overline{)22{,}444}$

11. $45\overline{)43{,}335}$

3. $25\overline{)31{,}375}$

6. $40\overline{)30{,}000}$

9. $89\overline{)56{,}070}$

12. $18\overline{)62{,}298}$

Solve each word problem. Show your work and write the answer in the space provided.

1. Travis had a birthday party and invited 26 friends. He had 390 baseball cards to give as party favors. How many baseball cards did each friend receive if Travis gave away all of his cards?

2. Terrance is reading a book about computers. There are 882 pages in the book. Terrance wants to finish the book in 2 weeks. How many pages does he need to read each day to finish the book within his deadline?

3. Susan has 560 different horse figures. She has 16 shelves on which to place her figures. How many horses will go on each shelf?

4. Gail needed more room in her closet. She decided to take half of her outfits and place them in the attic closet. She had a total of 42 outfits. How many outfits were moved to the attic?

5. Jason went to the store to buy candy for his classmates. There are 36 students in his homeroom. He bought a bag of candy that has 1,620 pieces inside. How many pieces will each classmate receive?

6. Anna's fourth grade class is planning a field trip to an amusement park. There are 29 students in her class. Each student must earn points to go on the trip. All 29 students must earn a total of 2,697 points. How many points must each student earn?

Total Problems: _____ Total Correct: _____ Score: _____

Study the box below. Divide each problem, making sure the remainder is less than the divisor. Then, write the answer in the space provided.

Rules:

1. Follow the steps of long division.

2. Compare the difference with the divisor. If it is larger, take more groups out of the dividend. If it is smaller, the number is the remainder.

Example:

$$4 \overline{)135} \quad \mathbf{33 \ R3}$$

$$-12$$

$$15 \qquad (R = remainder)$$

$$-12$$

$$3$$

---

1. $8 \overline{)489}$

4. $6 \overline{)576}$

7. $8 \overline{)6,312}$

10. $7 \overline{)2,537}$

2. $5 \overline{)921}$

5. $7 \overline{)234}$

8. $9 \overline{)8,329}$

11. $8 \overline{)1,778}$

3. $2 \overline{)835}$

6. $6 \overline{)379}$

9. $5 \overline{)3,400}$

12. $7 \overline{)1,652}$

Total Problems: _____ **Total Correct:** _____ **Score:** _____

Study the example below. Estimate the quotients. Then, write the answer on the line provided.

Example:

$$116 \div 4 = \longrightarrow 120 \div 4 = \longrightarrow 120 \div 4 = \mathbf{30}$$

Round the dividend.   116 rounds to 120.   Use mental math to divide.

1. $631 \div 3 =$ _____

2. $224 \div 4 =$ _____

3. $654 \div 5 =$ _____

4. $486 \div 7 =$ _____

5. $709 \div 9 =$ _____

6. $386 \div 3 =$ _____

7. $427 \div 5 =$ _____

8. $283 \div 7 =$ _____

9. $162 \div 8 =$ _____

10. $628 \div 9 =$ _____

11. $438 \div 2 =$ _____

12. $981 \div 4 =$ _____

13. $656 \div 2 =$ _____

14. $684 \div 4 =$ _____

15. $864 \div 4 =$ _____

16. $788 \div 5 =$ _____

17. $841 \div 7 =$ _____

18. $423 \div 2 =$ _____

19. $869 \div 5 =$ _____

20. $648 \div 5 =$ _____

21. $903 \div 3 =$ _____

22. $769 \div 7 =$ _____

23. $945 \div 5 =$ _____

24. $751 \div 6 =$ _____

Total Problems: **Total Correct:**   **Score:**

Divide. Write the quotient in the space provided.

1. 6)604

5. 6)788

9. 39)400

13. 5)4,672

2. 5)716

6. 4)791

10. 57)665

14. 7)4,347

3. 8)819

7. 8)977

11. 47)549

15. 8)5,789

4. 3)901

8. 3)987

12. 27)344

16. 8)63,456

| Total Problems: | Total Correct: | Score: |

Solve each word problem. Show your work and write the answer in the space provided.

---

1. Bruce earned $650.00 for delivering newspapers. He earned his money over 5 weeks. How much did he earn each week?

4. Susan goes to the gym every day. She wants to burn calories during her workout. She needs to burn 300 calories every hour. How many calories does Susan need to burn per minute?

---

2. Barbara wanted to knit 8 sweaters for each of her grandchildren. If Barbara knitted 120 sweaters during the entire year, how many grandchildren does Barbara have?

5. Fred has 24 friends that are coming to his Fourth of July party. He buys 144 cans of soda. How many cans of soda can each guest have?

---

3. Kameelah got a box of building blocks. The box had 789 blocks inside. If she made 3 towers with an equal amount of blocks, how many blocks were used to build each tower?

6. Owners from 11 different music companies have been invited to a music festival. Each owner brings a number of compact discs to the festival. If there were a total of 6,215 compact discs and each owner brought the same amount, how many compact discs did each owner bring?

Total Problems: _____   Total Correct: _____   Score: _____

Study the box below. For each problem, write a fraction which names the shaded part of each figure.

Rule:

A fraction names a part of the whole.

Example:

What part of the circle is shaded?

 $\dfrac{\text{1 part shaded}}{\text{out of 2 total parts}}$ is $\dfrac{1}{2}$

Since 1 out of 2 parts of the circle is shaded, $\dfrac{1}{2}$ would name the shaded part.

1.

_____ is shaded

5.

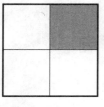

_____ is shaded

2.

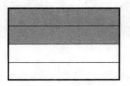

_____ is shaded

6.

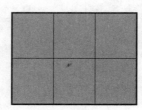

_____ is shaded

3.

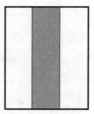

_____ is shaded

7.

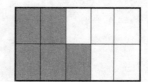

_____ is shaded

4.

_____ is shaded

8.

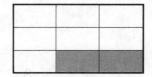

_____ is shaded

Total Problems: **Total Correct:** **Score:**

Study the box below. Then, for each pair of fractions, find the missing number that would make the pair equivalent. Write the answer in the space provided.

Rules:	**Example:**
Different fractions that name the same amount are **equivalent fractions**. To find an equivalent fraction, multiply both the numerator and the denominator by the same number.	$\dfrac{1}{3} = \dfrac{2}{6}$ $\dfrac{1\,(\times 2)}{3\,(\times 2)} = \dfrac{2}{6}$

1. $\dfrac{2}{4} = \dfrac{}{8}$

2. $\dfrac{1}{2} = \dfrac{}{16}$

3. $\dfrac{3}{9} = \dfrac{}{27}$

4. $\dfrac{}{4} = \dfrac{3}{12}$

5. $\dfrac{}{10} = \dfrac{14}{20}$

6. $\dfrac{}{15} = \dfrac{10}{30}$

7. $\dfrac{9}{11} = \dfrac{18}{}$

8. $\dfrac{4}{5} = \dfrac{16}{}$

9. $\dfrac{6}{8} = \dfrac{18}{}$

10. $\dfrac{3}{5} = \dfrac{}{25}$

11. $\dfrac{7}{8} = \dfrac{}{72}$

12. $\dfrac{8}{9} = \dfrac{}{81}$

13. $\dfrac{6}{} = \dfrac{12}{14}$

14. $\dfrac{1}{} = \dfrac{15}{30}$

15. $\dfrac{4}{} = \dfrac{36}{90}$

Total Problems: **Total Correct:**   **Score:**

Study the box below. Compare the fractions using <, >, or =. Then, place the correct symbol in each square.

Rule:

When comparing fractions with unlike denominators, follow these steps:

1. Look at the denominators to find a common multiple. This is the new denominator.

2. Multiply each numerator by the amount required to equal the new denominator. This is the new numerator for each fraction.

3. When the fractions have a common denominator, compare the numerators directly.

Example:

$$\frac{2}{5} \quad \square \quad \frac{3}{4}$$

$$\frac{2\ (\times 4)}{5\ (\times 4)} = \frac{8}{20} \qquad \frac{3\ (\times 5)}{4\ (\times 5)} = \frac{15}{20}$$

$$\frac{8}{20} \; < \; \frac{15}{20}$$

Since $\frac{8}{20} < \frac{15}{20}$, then $\frac{2}{5} < \frac{3}{4}$.

---

1. $\frac{1}{10} \; \square \; \frac{1}{8}$

2. $\frac{3}{10} \; \square \; \frac{2}{5}$

3. $\frac{1}{4} \; \square \; \frac{3}{10}$

4. $\frac{1}{2} \; \square \; \frac{5}{8}$

5. $\frac{2}{3} \; \square \; \frac{1}{2}$

6. $\frac{1}{2} \; \square \; \frac{4}{8}$

7. $\frac{1}{5} \; \square \; \frac{1}{4}$

8. $\frac{4}{10} \; \square \; \frac{1}{8}$

9. $\frac{5}{8} \; \square \; \frac{3}{4}$

10. $\frac{1}{2} \; \square \; \frac{1}{3}$

Total Problems: **Total Correct:**   **Score:**

Study the box below. Then, solve each problem and write the answer in the space provided.

Rules:	Examples:	
To find $\frac{1}{2}$ of a number, divide by 2.	$\frac{1}{2}$ of 20 is **10**.	$\frac{2}{5}$ of 15 is **6**.
To find $\frac{1}{3}$ of a number, divide by 3.	Since 20 ÷ 2 = 10, cutting 20 in half will give you 10.	Since 15 ÷ 5 = 3, 3 x 2 will give you 6.
To find $\frac{1}{4}$ of a number, divide by 4.		

1. $\frac{1}{5}$ of 20 =

2. $\frac{1}{4}$ of 16 =

3. $\frac{1}{2}$ of 14 =

4. $\frac{1}{8}$ of 24 =

5. $\frac{1}{3}$ of 18 =

6. $\frac{1}{3}$ of 24 =

7. $\frac{1}{2}$ of 12 =

8. $\frac{1}{4}$ of 4 =

9. $\frac{1}{2}$ of 8 =

10. $\frac{2}{5}$ of 20 =

11. $\frac{1}{5}$ of 25 =

12. $\frac{3}{4}$ of 4 =

13. $\frac{2}{3}$ of 6 =

14. $\frac{2}{3}$ of 21 =

15. $\frac{3}{4}$ of 20 =

16. $\frac{2}{5}$ of 25 =

17. $\frac{3}{5}$ of 10 =

18. $\frac{4}{5}$ of 15 =

19. $\frac{2}{3}$ of 9 =

20. $\frac{3}{4}$ of 12 =

21. $\frac{3}{8}$ of 16 =

Total Problems: **Total Correct:**   **Score:**

Name _____

Study the box below. Then, solve each problem, paying careful attention to the sign. Write the answer in the space provided.

Rule:	Examples:
When adding or subtracting fractions with the same denominator:	$\dfrac{2}{10} + \dfrac{4}{10} = \dfrac{6}{10}$
1. Add or subtract their numerators.	
2. Write that number over the same denominator.	$\dfrac{9}{10} - \dfrac{3}{10} = \dfrac{6}{10}$

1. $\dfrac{2}{6} - \dfrac{1}{6} =$

2. $\dfrac{1}{4} + \dfrac{1}{4} =$

3. $\dfrac{4}{6} - \dfrac{2}{6} =$

4. $\dfrac{2}{4} + \dfrac{1}{4} =$

5. $\dfrac{1}{10} + \dfrac{5}{10} =$

6. $\dfrac{9}{10} - \dfrac{4}{10} =$

7. $\dfrac{1}{6} + \dfrac{4}{6} =$

8. $\dfrac{7}{8} - \dfrac{1}{8} =$

9. $\dfrac{3}{12} + \dfrac{4}{12} =$

10. $\dfrac{9}{8} - \dfrac{2}{8} =$

11. $\dfrac{2}{10} - \dfrac{1}{10} =$

12. $\dfrac{1}{10} + \dfrac{8}{10} =$

13. $\dfrac{15}{18} - \dfrac{8}{18} =$

14. $\dfrac{4}{8} + \dfrac{3}{8} =$

15. $\dfrac{8}{10} - \dfrac{5}{10} =$

16. $\dfrac{3}{6} + \dfrac{2}{6} =$

17. $\dfrac{8}{8} - \dfrac{2}{8} =$

18. $\dfrac{2}{16} + \dfrac{9}{16} =$

Total Problems:	Total Correct:	Score:

49

Name _____

Study the box below. Then, use equivalent fractions to find the sums or differences of the following problems. Write the answer in the space provided.

Rule:	Examples:	
When adding or subtracting fractions with different denominators:	$\frac{2}{4}$ (x 2) = $\frac{4}{8}$	$\frac{3}{5}$ (x 2) = $\frac{6}{10}$
1. Look at the denominators.	$+\ \frac{5}{8}$ (x 1) = $\frac{5}{8}$	$-\ \frac{1}{10}$ (x 1) = $\frac{1}{10}$
2. Find the equivalent fractions.		
3. Add or subtract the new fractions.	$\frac{9}{8} = 1\frac{1}{8}$	$\frac{5}{10} = \frac{1}{2}$
4. If necessary, convert the fraction to a mixed number.		

1. $\frac{3}{8}$ =

   $+\ \frac{3}{4}$ =
   _____

4. $\frac{5}{8}$ =

   $-\ \frac{1}{4}$ =
   _____

7. $\frac{2}{5}$ =

   $+\ \frac{1}{10}$ =
   _____

2. $\frac{7}{8}$ =

   $-\ \frac{1}{2}$ =
   _____

5. $\frac{3}{10}$ =

   $+\ \frac{1}{5}$ =
   _____

8. $\frac{5}{8}$ =

   $-\ \frac{1}{2}$ =
   _____

3. $\frac{1}{4}$ =

   $+\ \frac{3}{8}$ =
   _____

6. $\frac{5}{6}$ =

   $-\ \frac{1}{3}$ =
   _____

9. $\frac{3}{4}$ =

   $+\ \frac{1}{2}$ =
   _____

Total Problems: _____ Total Correct: _____ Score: _____

Study the box below. Multiply each problem and write the answer in the space provided.

Rule:	**Example:**
1. Multiply the numerators.	$\dfrac{2}{3} \times \dfrac{3}{4} = \dfrac{6}{12}$
2. Multiply the denominators.	
3. Write the new fraction.	

1. $\dfrac{5}{6} \times \dfrac{1}{4} =$

2. $\dfrac{1}{4} \times \dfrac{1}{8} =$

3. $\dfrac{1}{9} \times \dfrac{1}{9} =$

4. $\dfrac{5}{8} \times \dfrac{3}{4} =$

5. $\dfrac{5}{9} \times \dfrac{2}{3} =$

6. $\dfrac{3}{4} \times \dfrac{3}{4} =$

7. $\dfrac{7}{8} \times \dfrac{5}{6} =$

8. $\dfrac{3}{8} \times \dfrac{2}{5} =$

9. $\dfrac{5}{6} \times \dfrac{1}{6} =$

10. $\dfrac{2}{3} \times \dfrac{1}{3} =$

11. $\dfrac{6}{7} \times \dfrac{1}{4} =$

12. $\dfrac{5}{12} \times \dfrac{5}{8} =$

13. $\dfrac{2}{3} \times \dfrac{11}{12} =$

14. $\dfrac{3}{5} \times \dfrac{8}{9} =$

15. $\dfrac{6}{10} \times \dfrac{1}{3} =$

16. $\dfrac{6}{8} \times \dfrac{4}{8} =$

17. $\dfrac{5}{7} \times \dfrac{4}{9} =$

18. $\dfrac{2}{4} \times \dfrac{2}{5} =$

Total Problems:	Total Correct:	Score:

Study the box below. Write a mixed number for each fraction. Write the answer in the space provided.

Rule:		Example:
1. Divide the numerator by the denominator.		
2. Write the quotient as the whole number.	$\dfrac{19}{3} \longrightarrow$	$\begin{array}{r} 6\ R1 \\ 3\overline{)\ 19} \\ -18 \\ \hline 1 \end{array}$ $6\dfrac{1}{3}$
3. The remainder is written as the numerator over the denominator (divisor).		

1. $\dfrac{37}{5} =$

2. $\dfrac{17}{2} =$

3. $\dfrac{11}{4} =$

4. $\dfrac{27}{4} =$

5. $\dfrac{11}{3} =$

6. $\dfrac{35}{4} =$

7. $\dfrac{15}{4} =$

8. $\dfrac{19}{6} =$

9. $\dfrac{29}{3} =$

10. $\dfrac{23}{6} =$

11. $\dfrac{19}{2} =$

12. $\dfrac{9}{4} =$

13. $\dfrac{71}{8} =$

14. $\dfrac{36}{5} =$

15. $\dfrac{39}{7} =$

16. $\dfrac{13}{2} =$

17. $\dfrac{22}{3} =$

18. $\dfrac{15}{6} =$

Total Problems: **Total Correct:**   **Score:**

Study the box below. Write an improper fraction for each mixed number. Write the answer in the space provided.

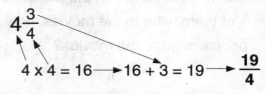

Rule:

1. Multiple the denominator and the whole number.

2. Add the numerator to the product.

3. Place the answer over the denominator.

Example:

$4\frac{3}{4}$

$4 \times 4 = 16 \longrightarrow 16 + 3 = 19 \longrightarrow \frac{19}{4}$

1. $2\frac{3}{4} =$

2. $6\frac{4}{7} =$

3. $4\frac{5}{6} =$

4. $8\frac{2}{4} =$

5. $10\frac{4}{8} =$

6. $7\frac{2}{5} =$

7. $3\frac{5}{8} =$

8. $9\frac{3}{9} =$

9. $4\frac{2}{3} =$

10. $5\frac{1}{5} =$

11. $1\frac{3}{4} =$

12. $2\frac{3}{8} =$

13. $6\frac{7}{9} =$

14. $3\frac{2}{5} =$

15. $5\frac{2}{7} =$

16. $4\frac{1}{2} =$

17. $7\frac{3}{4} =$

18. $1\frac{7}{8} =$

Total Problems: **Total Correct:**   **Score:**

Solve each word problem. Show your work and write the answer in the space provided.

---

1. There are 6 people in the Morris family. If $\frac{1}{3}$ of them went to the movies, how many people went to the movies?

4. A beaver footprint is $6\frac{4}{8}$ inches long. A cat footprint is $2\frac{4}{8}$ inches long. How much longer is the beaver print than the cat print?

---

2. Two-fourths of Miss Moore's class looked for rocks. How many students of Miss Moore's 24 students searched for rocks?

5. Roger ate $\frac{1}{4}$ of the pumpkin pie. Bruce ate $\frac{1}{3}$ of the same pie. How much of the pie was left after Roger and Bruce ate their pieces?

---

3. Pia bought her cat at the pet shop for half as much as the price of the Smith family kittens. If the Smith family was selling each kitten for $15.00, how much did Pia pay at the pet shop?

6. Dora walked $2\frac{1}{2}$ miles on Monday. Lisa walked twice as many miles as Dora. How many miles did Dora and Lisa walk altogether?

    Total Problems: **Total Correct:**   **Score:**

Study the examples below. Then, write the decimal for each problem in the space provided.

Examples:

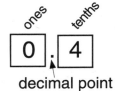

0.4 = four-tenths | 0.41 = forty-one-hundredths

decimal point

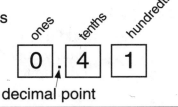

decimal point

1. one-tenth	**5.** three and four-tenths	**9.** ten and ten-tenths
2. nineteen-hundredths	**6.** eighty-six-hundredths	**10.** fourteen-hundredths
3. four-hundredths	**7.** twelve and four-hundredths	**11.** sixty-four-hundredths
4. five and six-hundredths	**8.** eight-hundredths	**12.** nine-tenths

Study the examples below. Then, write each decimal in words in the space provided.

Examples:

4.8 = **four and eight-tenths**   3.45 = **three and forty-five-hundredths**

13. 3.25	**18.** .89	**23.** 14.1
14. 5.2	**19.** 1.01	**24.** .55
15. .2	**20.** .25	**25.** .69
16. 95.26	**21.** .16	**26.** 7.8
17. 2.2	**22.** 25.12	**27.** 3.0

Total Problems: **Total Correct:**   **Score:**   **55**

Name _____

Study the examples below. Add or subtract each problem and write the answer in the space provided. Rewrite any horizontal problem as a vertical problem, lining up the decimals.

Examples:

$8.6 + 1.42 =$

```
   8.60
 + 1.42
 ------
  10.02
```
Add a 0 to fill in the empty space.
Line up the decimal points.

$3.1 - 2.18 =$

```
  2 1010
   3̶.1̶0̶
 - 2.18
 ------
   0.92
```
Add a 0 to fill in the empty space.
Line up the decimal points.

---

1. $6.4 + 9.3 =$

6. $4.68 + 6.7 =$

11. $8.68 - 3.7 =$

16. $9.92 - 7.1 =$

2.
```
   2.83
 + 1.39
```

7.
```
   5.3
 - 2.1
```

12.
```
   0.52
 + 0.37
```

17. $43.8 + 14.12 =$

3. $3.7 - 2.8 =$

8. $1.2 + 0.3 =$

13.
```
   4.24
 + 2.95
```

18.
```
   4.8
 - 3.7
```

4.
```
   43.8
 +  9.4
```

9. $95.6 - 82.12 =$

14. $6.8 - 2.5 =$

19. $3.45 + 6.49 =$

5.
```
   5.9
 - 4.4
```

10.
```
   0.36
 + 0.87
```

15.
```
   2.7
 + 8.9
```

20.
```
   16.10
 - 13.05
```

56

Total Problems: _____ **Total Correct:** _____ **Score:** _____

Name _____

Study the box below. Multiply each problem and write the answer in the space provided. Be sure to include a decimal point in the answer.

Rule:	Example:
1. Multiply as you would with whole numbers. 2. Count the number of digits to the right of the decimal point. 3. The product should have the same number of digits to the right of the decimal point.	3.7 x 6 ——— 222 Multiply, then count the number of digits to the right of the decimal point. 3.7 x 6 ——— **22.2**

1.   2.8
   x   6

2.   3.09
   x   5

3.   8.3
   x   4

4.   6.25
   x   3

5.   97.44
   x   7

6.   6.2
   x   8

7.   5.14
   x   8

8.   5.3
   x   6

9.   79.9
   x   6

10.   8.7
   x   8

11.   14.3
   x   6

12.   53
   x   .4

13.   139
   x   .6

14.   124
   x   .8

15.   49.5
   x   4

16.   7.65
   x   3

17.   3.8
   x   5

18.   9.98
   x   8

19.   10.5
   x   5

20.   162
   x   .9

Total Problems: **Total Correct:**   **Score:**

Solve each word problem. Show your work, paying attention to the placement of the decimal points. Then, write the answer in the space provided.

1. Dallas, Texas, had 49.52 cm of snow one year. The next year only 8.59 cm of snow fell. What was the difference in snowfall in the 2 years?	4. A group of bikers took 3 hours to go from the North Entrance to the South Entrance of Mead Park. The distance one way was 20.6 miles. About how far did they travel each hour?
2. Atlanta, Georgia, had 78.43 cm of rain one year. The following year 89.54 cm of rain fell. How much rain did Atlanta have in the 2 years together?	5. Mr. Abram has 9 water heaters for his apartment buildings. Each heater weighs 31.75 kilograms. How much do all 9 heaters weigh together?
3. There are 17.9 grams of protein in a serving of chicken. The same size serving of fish has 25.2 grams of protein. How much more protein does the fish have?	6. Terrance paid $985.00 for a couch. He bought a matching chair for $395.52. How much more was the couch?

Total Problems: ___ Total Correct: ___ Score: ___

Find each time. All times for problems 1–6 are P.M. Write the answer on the line provided.

1. 20 minutes later

_____

3. 55 minutes earlier

_____

5. 30 minutes later

_____

2. 45 minutes later

_____

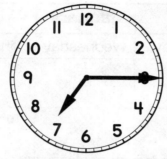

4. 15 minutes earlier

_____

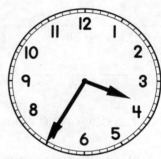

6. 55 minutes earlier

_____

Find each time. Write the answer on the line provided.

7. What time is 15 minutes after 9:05 A.M.?

_____

8. What time is 2 hours and 5 minutes before 2:15 P.M.?

_____

9. What time will it be 1 hour and 25 minutes after 3:35 P.M.?

_____

10. How much time has elapsed between 3:35 P.M. and 7:45 P.M.?

_____

11. Add 15 minutes to 5:24 P.M. to get a new time.

_____

12. What is 25 minutes before 11:45 A.M.?

_____

| Total Problems: | Total Correct: | Score: |

Name _____

Use the calendar to answer the following questions. Then, write the answer on the line provided.

January						
Sunday	Monday	Tuesday	Wednesday	Thursday	Friday	Saturday
		1	2	3	4	5
6	7	8	9	10	11	12
13	14	15	16	17	18	19
20	21	22	23	24	25	26
27	28	29	30	31		

1. What day of the week is January 16? _____

2. What is the date of the third Tuesday? _____

3. How many Sundays are in the month? _____

4. What day of the week is January 9? _____

5. What day and date is exactly 9 days from the 15? _____

6. What is the date of the first Friday? _____

7. What day of the week will February 1 be? _____

8. How many Saturdays are there in the month? _____

9. What day of the week is January 29? _____

10. On what date does the beginning of the third week fall? _____

60

Total Problems: _____ Total Correct: _____ Score: _____

Name _____

Solve each word problem. Show your work and write the answer in the space provided.

---

1. Mark left his house at 8:15 A.M. He was at work for 9 hours and 45 minutes. At what time did he return?

---

2. Meg started her workout session at 5:30 P.M. It lasted 65 minutes. What time did she finish?

---

3. Mr. Walters rode the bus to the stadium at 4:25 P.M. He returned that night at 11:35 P.M. How long was he gone?

---

4. Chandra planned a business trip every Tuesday for an entire month. There were 30 days in the month, and her first trip was on the third. How many trips did she make that month?

---

5. Reggie went to bed at 9:30 P.M. If he slept for 8 hours, when did he wake up the next morning?

---

6. Monica wants to go to the ball game and to the movies. The ball game begins at 2:15 P.M. and lasts for 3 hours. The movie is at 5:00 P.M. Will she be able to attend both events the same day?

---

7. Sally began playing golf at 9:15 A.M. She played for 3 hours and took a break. She resumed playing at 2:00 P.M. and played until 5:00 that evening. How many hours in all did she play golf?

---

8. Mrs. Jackson sends a postcard to her grandson every month on the 15th. If she does this for a full year, how many postcards will he receive in all?

Total Problems:	Total Correct:	Score:

Study the examples below. Complete each problem. Remember to line up the decimal points. Rewrite any horizontal problem vertically. Then, write the answer in the space provided.

Examples:	
$14.38 − $6.32 =	$13.01 + $10.62 =
$14.38	$13.01
− $6.32	+ $10.62
$ 8.06	**$23.63**

1. $38.42 + $16.45 =

5. $54.41 − $10.01 =

9. $980.25 − $42.21 =

2. $36.14 − $16.44 =

6. $49.38 + $114.69 =

10. $883.74 + $16.52 =

3.
$142.36
− $16.49

7.
$76.16
− $20.98

11.
$95.88
+ $29.71

4.
$16.42
+ $3.76

8.
$46.38
− $14.72

12.
$600.00
− $217.15

Total Problems: **Total Correct:**   **Score:**

Study the box below. Complete each problem. Be sure to place the numbers in the correct place value and watch the placement of the decimal point. Write the answer in the space provided.

Rules:

Multiplication: Count the number of digits to the right of the decimal point. The product should have the same number of digits to the right of the decimal point.

Division: Place the decimal point in the quotient. It goes in the same place as in the dividend.

Examples:

$16.32
x   14
6528
1632
$228.48

$$\begin{array}{r} 3.76 \\ 4\overline{)\$15.04} \\ -12 \\ \hline 30 \\ -28 \\ \hline 24 \\ -24 \\ \hline 0 \end{array}$$

---

1. $13.96
   x   5

2. $18.79
   x   8

3. $42.36
   x   12

4. $92.82
   x   21

5. $18.42
   x   10

6. $73.56
   x   32

7. $4\overline{)\$113.96}$

8. $6\overline{)\$149.94}$

9. $12\overline{)\$171.24}$

Study the examples below. Estimate the sums and differences of money. Write the dollar sign and the decimal point in the answer in the space provided.

Examples:

Round to the nearest $0.10:	Round to the nearest $1.00:	Round to the nearest $10.00:
$0.85 ⟶ $0.90	$8.39 ⟶ $8.00	$34.60 ⟶ $30.00
+ $0.29 ⟶ + $0.30	− $2.75 ⟶ − $3.00	+ $47.30 ⟶ +$50.00
$1.20	**$5.00**	**$80.00**

1. $24.98
  + $83.75

5. $26.75
  − $19.83

9. $7.74
  − $5.46

2. $49.64
    $26.05
  + $73.02

6. $38.74
    $29.07
  + $56.86

10. $18.25
    $14.45
  + $6.56

3. $0.46 + $0.43 + $0.27 =

7. $9.45 − $1.63 =

11. $45.78 − $26.09 =

4. $0.53 + $0.28 =

8. $6.59 + $8.25 + $1.45 =

12. $0.56 − $0.33 =

Total Problems: **Total Correct:**   **Score:**

Solve each word problem. Show your work and write the dollar sign and the decimal point in each answer in the space provided.

1. Kathleen had $15.00 to spend at the fair. She bought a hot dog and soda for $4.20. Kathleen spent $6.25 on a souvenir. How much money does Kathleen have after her purchases?

4. John spent $4.75 on food at the baseball game. He spent $13.27 on a souvenir hat. How much more did he spend on the food than on the hat?

2. Glen went to the store to buy items for his birthday party. He spent $14.23 on balloons and $28.32 for food. How much did Glen spend in all?

5. Lisa earned $31.36 each week for delivering newspapers. She delivered newspapers for 2 weeks. How much money did Lisa earn after 2 weeks?

3. Last year, Jimmy earned $413.29 by selling his prize-winning carrot cake at the Georgia State Fair. This year, he earned $592.56. How much more did Jimmy earn this year?

6. Brittani wants to buy 2 shirts that are on sale. Each shirt is on sale for $14.50 including tax. If Brittani has $30.00, how much change will she get after purchasing 2 shirts?

Study the rules below. Then, write the answer on the line provided.

Rules:

Length	Weight
10 millimeters (mm) = 1 centimeter (cm)	1 gram (g) = 1,000 milligrams (mg)
100 cm = 1 meter (m)	1,000 g = 1 kilogram (kg)
1,000 m = 1 kilometer (km)	

1. 2 meters = _____ centimeters

2. 3,200 grams = _____ kilograms

3. 20 centimeters = _____ millimeters

4. 8 kilograms = _____ grams

Choose the appropriate unit of measurement. Circle the letter beside the correct answer.

5. weight of a gold bracelet

   A. kilograms   C. millimeters

   B. grams   D. kilometers

6. length of a kitchen table

   A. millimeters   C. grams

   B. meters   D. kilograms

7. length of a pencil

   A. centimeters   C. grams

   B. meters   D. kilograms

8. weight of a dump truck

   A. kilograms   C. centimeters

   B. grams   D. kilometers

9. weight of an orange

   A. millimeters   C. kilograms

   B. grams   D. centimeters

10. length of chalkboard

   A. meters   C. centimeters

   B. kilometers   D. millimeters

66

Total Problems: _____   Total Correct: _____   Score: _____

Study the rules below. Choose the unit that makes the statement reasonable. Then, write the answer on the line provided.

Rules:

Length	Weight
1 foot (ft) = 12 inches (in)	16 ounces (oz) = 1 pound (lb)
1 yard (yd) = 3 ft = 36 in	2,000 lb = 1 ton
1 mile (mi) = 1,760 yd = 5,280 ft	

1. The football field is 100 _____ long.

2. A milk truck weighs 4 _____.

3. The teacher's desk is 30 _____ high.

4. An apple weighs 8 _____.

5. It is 45 _____from Millersville to Bakerstown. The drive takes about 1 hour.

6. Jennifer's new compact disk weighs 6 _____.

7. The ceiling in our classroom is 3 _____ high.

8. Mark's mother's new gold necklace weighs 2 _____.

9. Susan's father is about 6 _____ tall.

10. Kayla's grandfather weighs 185 _____.

Total Problems:	Total Correct:	Score:

Study the rules below. Choose the best unit of measurement. Circle the letter beside the correct answer.

> **Rules:**
>
> 2 cups = 1 pint (pt) | 4 qt = 1 gallon (gal)
>
> 2 pt = 1 quart (qt) | 16 cups = 1 gal

1. bowl of soup

  A. cup   C. quart

  B. pint   D. gallon

4. water in a bathtub

  A. cup   C. quart

  B. pint   D. gallon

2. glass of juice

  A. cup   C. quart

  B. pint   D. gallon

5. pitcher of water

  A. cup   C. quart

  B. pint   D. gallon

3. A filled baby pool

  A. cup   C. quart

  B. pint   D. gallon

6. motor oil

  A. cup   C. quart

  B. pint   D. gallon

Study the example below. Then, write the answer on the line provided.

> **Example:**
>
> 8 pints = _____ cups
>
> 1 pint equals 2 cups.
>
> 8 x 2 = 16 $\longrightarrow$ 8 pints = **16** cups

7. 5 quarts = _____ pints

8. 4 cups = _____ pints

9. _____ gallons = 16 pints

10. _____ pints = 2 quarts

11. 3 gallons = _____ pints

12. 2 pints = _____ cups

13. 5 gallons = _____ quarts

14. 3 quarts = _____ cups

Total Problems:	Total Correct:	Score:

Solve each word problem. Show your work and write the answer in the space provided.

---

1. Sally Rose made 8 quarts of punch for the birthday party. How many cups was that?

4. Mrs. Lackey wanted to give each child in her room a calculator. Each calculator weighed 16 ounces. If Mrs. Lackey gave each of her 20 students a calculator, how many pounds did the calculators weigh in all?

---

2. Two boxes of gold weigh 4 pounds 8 ounces. Each pound costs $400.00. How much are the boxes worth?

5. Virginia's school ordered 20 boxes of milk. In each box there were 35 containers of milk. On the last day, 265 containers were used. How many were left over?

---

3. Years ago, containers were used to measure milk. If 4 containers equaled 1 quart, how many quarts of milk was 184 containers?

6. If a chef uses 10 cups of whole wheat flour for each 12 cups of white enriched flour, how many cups of white enriched flour are needed to go with 30 cups of whole wheat flour?

Study the box below. Name each polygon. Tell how many sides and vertices there are. Write the answers on the lines provided.

Rule:	Example:
A **polygon** is a closed plane figure with 3 or more sides. A closed figure is a figure that has no open line segments. You can trace a line around the perimeter of a closed figure without ever coming to an end. The **vertex** is the point where 2 sides meet. More than 1 vertex is called **vertices**.	This is a quadrilateral with 4 sides and 4 vertices. 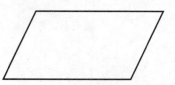

1.
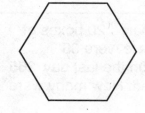
____ sides ____ vertices

4.
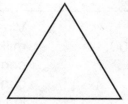
____ sides ____ vertices

7.
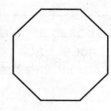
____ sides ____ vertices

2.

____ sides ____ vertices

5.
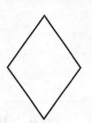
____ sides ____ vertices

8.
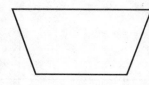
____ sides ____ vertices

3.

____ sides ____ vertices

6.
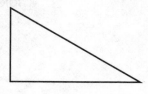
____ sides ____ vertices

9.
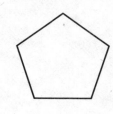
____ sides ____ vertices

Total Problems: _____ Total Correct: _____ Score: _____

Study the box below. Draw the line of symmetry on the following figures.

Rule:
A figure has a line of symmetry if it can be folded so that the two parts fit exactly (congruent).

Example:
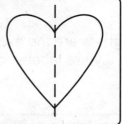

1.
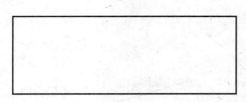

3.

2.

4.
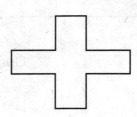

Does the dashed line in each figure represent the line of symmetry? Check each answer yes or no.

5.
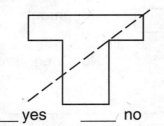
____ yes   ____ no

7.
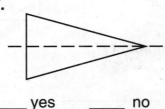
____ yes   ____ no

9.
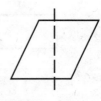
____ yes   ____ no

6.
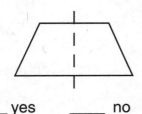
____ yes   ____ no

8.
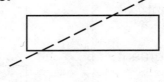
____ yes   ____ no

10.

____ yes   ____ no

Total Problems: _____   Total Correct: _____   Score: _____

Study the box below. Decide if each pair is congruent. Then, circle the correct answer.

Rule:	Example:
When figures are the exact same size and shape, they are labeled congruent.	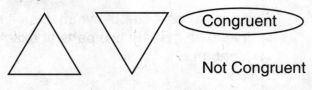

1.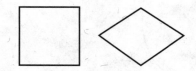

Congruent

Not Congruent

2.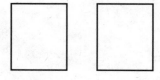

Congruent

Not Congruent

3.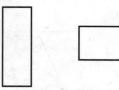

Congruent

Not Congruent

4.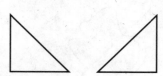

Congruent

Not Congruent

5.

Congruent

Not Congruent

6.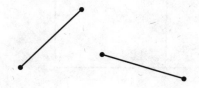

Congruent

Not Congruent

7.

Congruent

Not Congruent

8.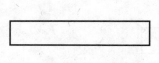

Congruent

Not Congruent

Total Problems:	Total Correct:	Score:

Name _____   **Lines, Line Segments, and Rays**

Study the examples below. Identify each figure as a line, line segment, or ray. Be sure to label the figures with the correct symbols. Write the answer on the line provided.

Examples:

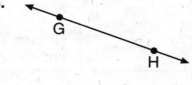

$\overleftrightarrow{AB}$ = Line AB (or BA)

$\overline{AB}$ = Line Segment AB (or BA)

$\overrightarrow{AB}$ = Ray AB

1.

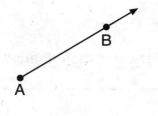

____ = ____

5.

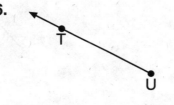

____ = ____

9.

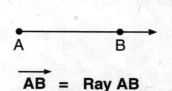

____ = ____

2.

____ = ____

6.

____ = ____

10.

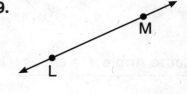

____ = ____

3.

____ = ____

7.

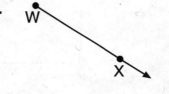

____ = ____

11.

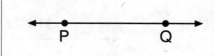

____ = ____

4.

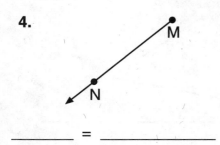

____ = ____

8.

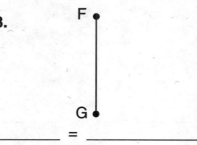

____ = ____

12.

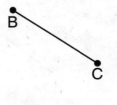

____ = ____

© Carson-Dellosa CD-2211

| Total Problems: | Total Correct: | Score: |

73

Study the examples below. Identify each angle as a right angle, straight angle, acute angle, or obtuse angle. Write the answer on the line provided.

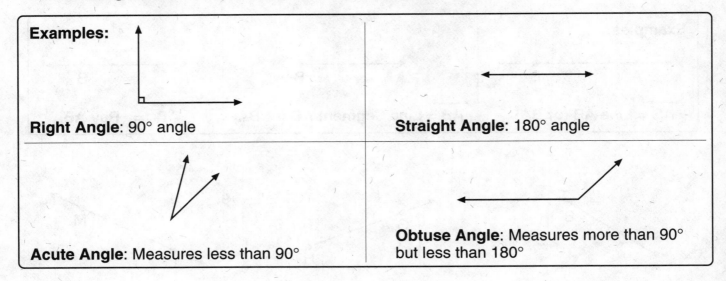

Examples:

Right Angle: 90° angle

Straight Angle: 180° angle

Acute Angle: Measures less than 90°

Obtuse Angle: Measures more than 90° but less than 180°

1.

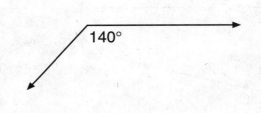
95°

_____

4.

140°

_____

2.

110°

_____

5.

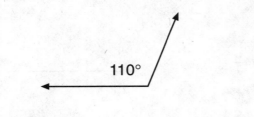
90°

_____

3.

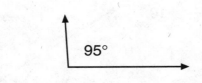
14°

_____

6.

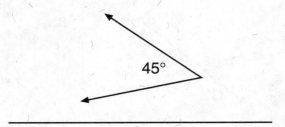
45°

_____

Total Problems: _____   Total Correct: _____   Score: _____

Study the box below. Find the perimeter of each figure. Then, write the answer in the space provided.

Rule:

The **perimeter** is the total distance around each figure.

To find the perimeter, add the lengths of all sides.

Example:

25 cm

4 cm [   ] 4 cm

25 cm

25 + 4 + 25 + 4 = **58 cm**

1.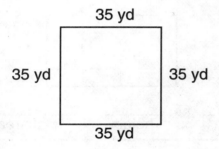

35 yd / 35 yd / 35 yd / 35 yd

2.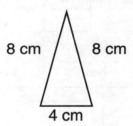

8 cm / 8 cm / 4 cm

3.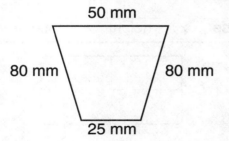

50 mm / 80 mm / 80 mm / 25 mm

4.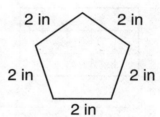

2 in / 2 in / 2 in / 2 in / 2 in

5.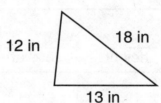

12 in / 18 in / 13 in

6.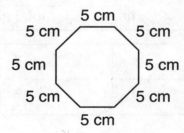

5 cm / 5 cm / 5 cm / 5 cm / 5 cm / 5 cm / 5 cm / 5 cm

Study the box below. Find the area of each figure. Write the answer on the line provided.

Rule:

The **area** is the number of square units inside a figure.

To find the area of rectangles and squares, multipy the **base** and the **height** (length times width).

Example:

2 square units

3 square units

Three square units times 2 square units equals an area of 6 square units.

(3 x 2 = **6 square units**)

1.

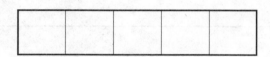

_____ x _____ = _____
base   height   total area

5.

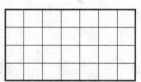

_____ x _____ = _____
base   height   total area

2.

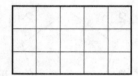

_____ x _____ = _____
base   height   total area

6.

_____ x _____ = _____
base   height   total area

3.

_____ x _____ = _____
base   height   total area

7.

_____ x _____ = _____
base   height   total area

4.

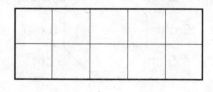

_____ x _____ = _____
base   height   total area

8.

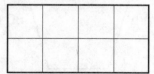

_____ x _____ = _____
base   height   total area

Total Problems: _____   Total Correct: _____   Score: _____

Study the table below. Use the information to answer each question. Write the answer on the line provided.

Student Music Lesson Schedule

DAY 1 (new students only)	DAY 2	DAY 3	DAY 4	DAY 5
Nicole	José	Solina	Greg	Jamie
Naomi	Kira	Jamie	Kipley	Solina
Tanya	Kipley	Greg	Jacob	Rebecca
Michelle	Mark	Rebecca	José	Mark
Fiora	Jacob	Margaret	Kira	Drake

1. When does Nicole have her music lesson? _____

2. Other than Jacob, who has a lesson on day 4? _____

3. Tanya, Naomi, and Fiora all have a lesson on which day? _____

4. When is Drake's lesson? _____

5. How many lessons is Jacob scheduled for in all? _____

6. Kipley, Naomi, and Mark practice together. Who is the new music student? _____

7. How many new students are there? _____

8. What days does Jamie have lessons? _____

9. When is Fiora's lesson? _____

10. Why do you think Mark does not have a lesson on day 1? _____

_____

Total Problems:	Total Correct:	Score:

Study the bar graph below. Use the information to answer each question on the
line provided.

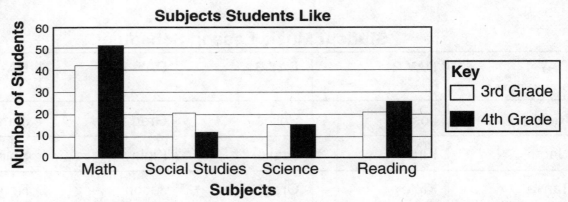

1. Which grade level liked math better?

    _____

2. Which subject did both grade levels like
    equally?

    _____

3. Which grade level like reading better?

    _____

4. What is the most popular subject in
    these grades?

    _____

Study the pictograph below. Use the information to answer each question on the
line provided.

Tires Sold

Month	Number of Tires Sold
Jan.	⬤ ⬤ ⬤ ⬤ ⬤ ◠
Feb.	⬤ ⬤
March	⬤ ◠
April	⬤ ⬤ ⬤ ◠
May	⬤

Key
⬤ = 500 tires

5. How many more tires were sold in April
    than in February?

    _____

6. What is the difference between the least
    number of tires sold and the greatest
    number of tires sold?

    _____

Total Problems: _____   Total Correct: _____   Score: _____

Place Value

Name _____ Place Value

Study the example below. Write the value of each underlined digit on the line provided.

Example:

	Millions			Thousands			Ones	
Hundred Millions	Ten Millions	Millions	Hundred Thousands	Ten Thousands	Thousands	Hundreds	Tens	Ones
5	0	3,	6	7	3,	9	8	2

The underlined digit **9** is in the hundreds place; therefore, it has a value of **900**.

1. 47<u>3</u>
   __70__

2. 2,0<u>7</u>5
   __5__

3. 2<u>8</u>,365
   __8,000__

4. 8<u>3</u>0,724
   __30,000__

5. <u>1</u>15,307
   __100,000__

6. <u>4</u>,781,326
   __4,000,000__

7. <u>9</u>4,320,188
   __90,000,000__

8. 133,2<u>7</u>8,245
   __30,000,000__

9. 6<u>4</u>9,228,713
   __9,000,000__ (*note: value shown*)

10. <u>1</u>47,306,254
    __100,000,000__

11. 4<u>6</u>,598
    __40,000__

12. <u>3</u>74,129
    __3000,000__

13. <u>2</u>57,123,448
    __200,000,000__

14. <u>7</u>32,146,209
    __2,000,000__

Total Problems: ___ Total Correct: ___ Score: ___

© Carson-Dellosa CD-2211 **9**

Reading and Writing Numbers

Name _____ Reading and Writing Numbers

Study the box below. Then, write each number in standard numerical form on the line provided.

Rule:
A number is usually written using digits in the appropriate place value spots. This is called standard form.

Examples:
five thousand, two hundred fifty-one = **5,251**
twenty-two thousand, thirty-three = **22,033**

1. seventeen thousand, four hundred thirty-three =
   __17,433__

2. five thousand, eight hundred ninety-one =
   __5,891__

3. six thousand, twenty-five =
   __6,025__

4. three hundred forty-two thousand, six hundred eight =
   __342,608__

5. seven hundred twenty-one thousand, nine hundred four =
   __721,904__

6. one million, eight hundred twenty thousand, five hundred fifteen =
   __1,820,515__

7. one hundred million, forty-three thousand, sixteen =
   __100,043,016__

8. seventy-one million, eight hundred forty-one thousand, five hundred four =
   __71,841,504__

9. nine billion, eighty-three million, six hundred two thousand, five hundred =
   __9,083,602,500__

10. sixty-five million, eight hundred forty thousand, three =
    __65,840,003__

11. sixty one thousand, eight =
    __61,008__

12. ninety-five billion, eight hundred seventy-three million, two hundred thousand, five hundred ninety-two =
    __95,873,200,592__

10 Total Problems: ___ Total Correct: ___ Score: ___ © Carson-Dellosa CD-2211

Numbers in Expanded Form

Name _____ Numbers in Expanded Form

Study the examples below. Then, circle the letter beside the correct answer.

Examples:
3,000 + 100 + 20 + 8 = **3,128**
800,000 + 10,000 + 30 + 2 = **810,032**

1. 5,000 + 300 + 20 + 8 =
   A. 50,328
   (B.) 5,328
   C. 538
   D. 503,208

2. 800 + 30 + 6 =
   A. 8,036
   B. 8,306
   (C.) 836
   D. 386

3. 20,000 + 3,000 + 200 + 8 =
   A. 2,328
   B. 23,280
   C. 20,208
   (D.) 23,208

4. 80,000 + 1,000 + 50 + 6 =
   (A.) 81,056
   B. 8,560
   C. 8,156
   D. 80,506

5. 700,000 + 20,000 + 2,000, + 100 + 70 =
   (A.) 722,170
   B. 702,170
   C. 72,217
   D. 7,217

6. 4,000,000 + 800,000 + 60,000 + 20 =
   A. 4,086,020
   (B.) 4,860,020
   C. 486,020
   D. 408,620

7. 9,000,000 + 70,000 + 300 + 80 + 6 =
   A. 970,386
   (B.) 9,070,386
   C. 907,386
   D. 973,086

8. 50,000 + 6,000 + 800 + 90 =
   (A.) 56,890
   B. 5,689
   C. 50,689
   D. 56,809

© Carson-Dellosa CD-2211 Total Problems: ___ Total Correct: ___ Score: ___ **11**

Rounding to Tens and Hundreds

Name _____ Rounding to Tens and Hundreds

Study the box below. Round each number to 10, then 100. Then, write the answer on the line provided.

Rules:
Round numbers to the nearest 10 by checking the digit in the ones place value spot. If that digit is 5 or greater, round up to the next 10. If it is 4 or lower, keep the same 10.
Round numbers to the nearest 100 by checking the digit in the tens place value spot. If that digit is 5 or greater, round up to the next 10. If it is 4 or lower, keep the same 100.

Examples:
9,483 =
Nearest 10: **9,480**
Nearest 100: **9,500**

2,795 =
Nearest 10: **2,800**
Nearest 100: **2,800**

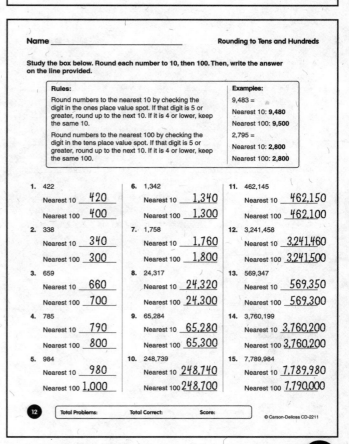

1. 422
   Nearest 10 __420__
   Nearest 100 __400__

2. 338
   Nearest 10 __340__
   Nearest 100 __300__

3. 659
   Nearest 10 __660__
   Nearest 100 __700__

4. 785
   Nearest 10 __790__
   Nearest 100 __800__

5. 984
   Nearest 10 __980__
   Nearest 100 __1,000__

6. 1,342
   Nearest 10 __1,340__
   Nearest 100 __1,300__

7. 1,758
   Nearest 10 __1,760__
   Nearest 100 __1,800__

8. 24,317
   Nearest 10 __24,320__
   Nearest 100 __24,300__

9. 65,284
   Nearest 10 __65,280__
   Nearest 100 __65,300__

10. 248,739
    Nearest 10 __248,740__
    Nearest 100 __248,700__

11. 462,145
    Nearest 10 __462,150__
    Nearest 100 __462,100__

12. 3,241,458
    Nearest 10 __3,241,460__
    Nearest 100 __3,241,500__

13. 569,347
    Nearest 10 __569,350__
    Nearest 100 __569,300__

14. 3,760,199
    Nearest 10 __3,760,200__
    Nearest 100 __3,760,200__

15. 7,789,984
    Nearest 10 __7,789,980__
    Nearest 100 __7,790,000__

12 Total Problems: ___ Total Correct: ___ Score: ___ © Carson-Dellosa CD-2211

Rounding Large Numbers

Name _____

Round to the nearest thousand. Then, write the answer on the line provided.

1. 5,384 ___5,000___
2. 7,521 ___8,000___
3. 8,432 ___8,000___
4. 62,381 ___62,000___
5. 76,432 ___76,000___
6. 82,197 ___82,000___
7. 94,306 ___94,000___
8. 738,149 ___738,000___

Round to the nearest million. Then, write the answer on the line provided.

9. 2,438,692 ___2,000,000___
10. 6,743,214 ___7,000,000___
11. 84,329,167 ___84,000,000___
12. 98,724,410 ___99,000,000___
13. 60,213,548 ___60,000,000___
14. 106,247,596 ___106,000,000___
15. 851,463,462 ___851,000,000___
16. 99,543,873 ___100,000,000___

Round to the nearest billion. Then, write the answer on the line provided.

17. 5,432,687,155 ___5,000,000,000___
18. 7,541,320,152 ___8,000,000,000___
19. 14,362,188,206 ___14,000,000,000___
20. 37,548,139,664 ___38,000,000,000___
21. 74,324,145,306 ___74,000,000,000___
22. 75,334,509,438 ___75,000,000,000___
23. 146,788,129,365 ___147,000,000,000___
24. 248,175,379,912 ___248,000,000,000___
25. 598,375,287,032 ___598,000,000,000___
26. 129,644,321,014 ___130,000,000,000___

© Carson-Dellosa CD-2211   Total Problems: ___ Total Correct: ___ Score: ___   **13**

Number Sense Problem Solving

Name _____

Solve each word problem. Then, write the answer in the space provided.

1. Write the number:
   Seven tens, five hundreds, six ones, seven thousands

   7,576

2. Write the number:
   Five thousand larger than twenty-five thousand

   30,000

3. Write the number:
   Eighty-thousand larger than four hundred twelve

   80,412

4. Write the number:
   Seven million less than twenty-one million, eight hundred forty-three thousand, six

   14,843,006

5. Write the larger number, using numerals.
   A. Sixty-four thousand, two hundred
   Ⓑ Four hundred three thousand, twelve

   403,012

6. Sam and Joseph went to the championship football game and saw twenty-eight thousand people. Write the number using numerals.

   28,000

7. Bobby and Janet flew 2,854 miles to their grandparents' house. Their cousins' flight was 13,492 miles. Who had farther to fly?

   their cousins

8. A company spent eight billion, eight million, ninety-five thousand dollars in one year for their employees. Write this number using numerals.

   $8,008,095,000

14   Total Problems: ___ Total Correct: ___ Score: ___   © Carson-Dellosa CD-2211

Basic Addition Facts

Name _____

Add. Then, write the sum on the line provided.

1. 4 + 8 = ___12___
2. 7 + 5 = ___12___
3. 9 + 9 = ___18___
4. 6 + 7 = ___13___
5. 8 + 3 = ___11___
6. 4 + 6 = ___10___
7. 5 + 9 = ___14___
8. 7 + 8 = ___15___
9. 5 + 8 = ___13___
10. 7 + 7 = ___14___
11. 9 + 2 = ___11___
12. 10 + 11 = ___21___
13. (4 + 2) + (8 + 1) = ___15___
14. 9 + (3 + 6) = ___18___
15. 9 + 7 + 3 = ___19___
16. 5 + (4 + 9) + 2 = ___20___
17. (8 + 6) + 3 = ___17___
18. (9 + 5) + (3 + 8) = ___25___
19. (7 + 1) + (8 + 8) = ___24___
20. 4 + 2 + 6 = ___12___
21. (3 + 3) + (8 + 9) = ___23___
22. (5 + 4) + (2 + 4) + 6 = ___21___
23. (7 + 9) + (5 + 5) = ___26___
24. (4 + 6) + (2 + 9) = ___21___

© Carson-Dellosa CD-2211   Total Problems: ___ Total Correct: ___ Score: ___   **15**

Comparing Sums

Name _____

Study the examples below. Use the comparison symbols >, <, or = to complete the number sentences below. Then, place the symbol in the square provided.

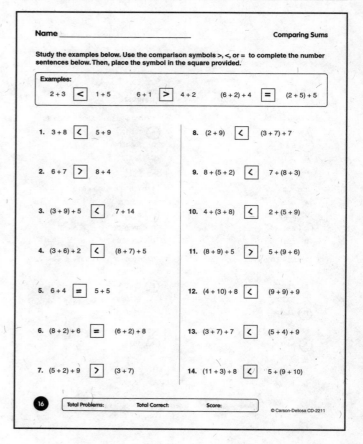

Examples:

2 + 3 [<] 1 + 5   6 + 1 [>] 4 + 2   (6 + 2) + 4 [=] (2 + 5) + 5

1. 3 + 8 [<] 5 + 9
2. 6 + 7 [>] 8 + 4
3. (3 + 9) + 5 [<] 7 + 14
4. (3 + 6) + 2 [<] (8 + 7) + 5
5. 6 + 4 [=] 5 + 5
6. (8 + 2) + 6 [=] (6 + 2) + 8
7. (5 + 2) + 9 [>] (3 + 7)
8. (2 + 9) [<] (3 + 7) + 7
9. 8 + (5 + 2) [<] 7 + (8 + 3)
10. 4 + (3 + 8) [<] 2 + (5 + 9)
11. (8 + 9) + 5 [>] 5 + (9 + 6)
12. (4 + 10) + 8 [<] (9 + 9) + 9
13. (3 + 7) + 7 [<] (5 + 4) + 9
14. (11 + 3) + 8 [<] 5 + (9 + 10)

16   Total Problems: ___ Total Correct: ___ Score: ___   © Carson-Dellosa CD-2211

Worksheet 17 — Addition with Regrouping

Name _____ Addition with Regrouping

Study the box below. Then, add and write the answer in the space provided.

Rule:	Example:
1. Add the ones column, then regroup.	217,388 + 692,438 = 6
2. Add the tens column, then regroup.	217,388 + 692,438 = 26
3. Add the hundreds column, then regroup.	217,388 + 692,438 = 826
4. Continue to add columns and regroup as needed.	217,388 + 692,438 = 9,826 / 09,826 / **909,826**

1. 15 + 6 = 21
2. 24 + 17 = 41
3. 18 + 13 = 31
4. 25 + 15 = 40
5. 48 + 29 = 77
6. 37 + 27 = 64
7. 59 + 26 = 85
8. 63 + 38 = 101
9. 65 + 39 = 104
10. 95 + 67 = 162
11. 73 + 58 = 131
12. 99 + 25 = 124
13. 112 + 48 = 160
14. 123 + 59 = 182
15. 238 + 76 = 314
16. 264 + 87 = 351

Total Problems: ___ Total Correct: ___ Score: ___   **17**

© Carson-Dellosa CD-2211

Worksheet 18 — Addition Practice

Name _____ Addition Practice

Add. Then, write the answer in the space provided.

1. 543 + 27 = 570
2. 684 + 175 = 859
3. 7,543 + 287 = 7,830
4. 9,492 + 1,368 = 10,860
5. 351 + 347 = 698
6. 3,764 + 2,883 = 6,647
7. 3,429 + 8,462 = 11,891
8. 76,182 + 34,245 = 110,427
9. 80,996 + 36,215 = 117,211
10. 23,648 + 41,295 = 64,943
11. 43,204 + 23,524 = 66,728
12. 68,242 + 35,254 = 103,496
13. 173,249 + 56,245 = 229,494
14. 324,159 + 278,634 = 602,793
15. 543,286 + 215,740 = 759,026
16. 49,320 + 36,249 = 85,569
17. 624,193 + 453,126 = 1,077,319
18. 753,091 + 773,256 = 1,526,347
19. 785,122 + 542,137 = 1,327,259
20. 85,911 + 28,347 = 114,258

18 Total Problems: ___ Total Correct: ___ Score: ___

© Carson-Dellosa CD-2211

Worksheet 19 — Estimating Sums

Name _____ Estimating Sums

Study the examples below. Round each addend to the greatest place value. Then, add and write the answer in the space provided.

Examples:	
59 rounds to 60 / + 32 rounds to + 30 = 90	476 rounds to 500 / + 35 rounds to + 40 = 540

1. 46 + 32 → 50 + 30 = 80
2. 56 + 75 → 60 + 80 = 140
3. 88 + 62 → 90 + 60 = 150
4. 125 + 73 → 100 + 70 = 170
5. 236 + 88 → 200 + 90 = 290
6. 565 + 217 → 600 + 200 = 800
7. 609 + 233 → 600 + 200 = 800
8. 1,753 + 258 → 2,000 + 300 = 2,300
9. 13,954 + 5,268 → 10,000 + 5,000 = 15,000
10. 25,694 + 15,507 → 30,000 + 20,000 = 50,000
11. 136,284 + 98,509 → 100,000 + 100,000 = 200,000
12. 248,139 + 176,905 → 200,000 + 200,000 = 400,000
13. 603,897 + 562,533 → 600,000 + 600,000 = 1,200,000
14. 375,218 + 188,273 → 400,000 + 200,000 = 600,000
15. 492,376 + 99,495 → 500,000 + 100,000 = 600,000

Total Problems: ___ Total Correct: ___ Score: ___   **19**

© Carson-Dellosa CD-2211

Worksheet 20 — Addition Problem Solving

Name _____ Addition Problem Solving

Solve each word problem. Show your work. Then, write the answer in the space provided.

1. Jason has 14 baseball cards in his collection. He buys 12 more. How many cards does Jason have now?
   14 + 12 = 26 cards

2. Stephanie walked 4 miles on Monday, 6 miles on Tuesday, and 7 miles on Wednesday for her school walk-a-thon. How many miles did she walk in all?
   4 + 6 + 7 = 17 miles

3. Scott played video games for 5 hours on Saturday. On Sunday, he played 4 hours longer than he did on Saturday. How many hours did Scott play video games in all?
   5 + 9 = 14 hours

4. Natalie practiced her violin for 3 hours on Thursday, 2 hours on Friday, and 1 hour on both Saturday and Sunday. How many hours did she practice in all?
   3 + 2 + 1 = 7 hours

5. Devon drove his new sports car 45 miles the first day, 72 miles the second day, and 31 miles the third day. How many miles did he drive his sports car in all?
   45 + 72 + 31 = 148 miles

6. The theater sold 462 tickets for the 4:00 P.M. show and 362 tickets for the 7:00 P.M. show. How many tickets were sold in all?
   462 + 362 = 824 tickets

20 Total Problems: ___ Total Correct: ___ Score: ___

© Carson-Dellosa CD-2211

Worksheet 1 (top left)

Name _____   Basic Subtraction Facts

Subtract. Write the answer on the line provided.

1. $9 - 5 =$ __4__
2. $8 - 3 =$ __5__
3. $7 - 2 =$ __5__
4. $10 - 6 =$ __4__
5. $12 - 6 =$ __6__
6. $6 - 4 =$ __2__
7. $8 - 6 =$ __2__
8. $9 - 6 =$ __3__
9. $11 - 6 =$ __5__
10. $13 - 7 =$ __6__
11. $15 - 9 =$ __6__
12. $18 - 5 =$ __13__

13. $(8 - 3) - 1 =$ __4__
14. $(6 - 2) - 4 =$ __0__
15. $9 - (18 - 13) =$ __4__
16. $(9 - 5) - (6 - 4) =$ __2__
17. $(12 - 5) - (8 - 3) =$ __2__
18. $(15 - 4) - (13 - 9) =$ __7__
19. $(16 - 8) - (9 - 4) =$ __3__
20. $(20 - 10) - (8 - 7) =$ __9__
21. $(40 - 10) - (30 - 15) =$ __15__
22. $(25 - 15) - (10 - 5) =$ __5__
23. $(18 - 5) - (16 - 10) =$ __7__
24. $(28 - 10) - (15 - 5) =$ __8__

Total Problems: Total Correct: Score: **21**

© Carson-Dellosa CD-2211

Worksheet 2 (top right)

Name _____   Subtraction with Regrouping

Study the box below. Subtract. Then, write the answer in the space provided.

Rule:
1. Regroup, then subtract the ones column.
2. Regroup, then subtract the tens column.
3. Regroup, then subract the hundreds column.
4. Continue to subtract columns and regroup as needed.

When you regroup, the number to the left is decreased by one.

Example:

$$342,535 - 147,079 = 6$$
$$342,535 - 147,079 = 56$$
$$342,535 - 147,079 = 456$$
$$342,535 - 147,079 = 5,456$$
$$342,535 - 147,079 = 95,456$$
$$342,535 - 147,079 = 195,456$$

1. $15 - 8 = 7$
2. $53 - 19 = 34$
3. $62 - 47 = 15$
4. $55 - 37 = 18$
5. $125 - 78 = 47$
6. $139 - 64 = 75$
7. $465 - 298 = 167$
8. $3,403 - 597 = 2,806$
9. $6,562 - 688 = 5,874$
10. $7,541 - 2,975 = 4,566$
11. $12,133 - 9,742 = 2,391$
12. $10,374 - 8,585 = 1,789$
13. $45,162 - 29,798 = 15,364$
14. $75,334 - 28,567 = 46,767$
15. $85,665 - 38,777 = 46,888$
16. $98,043 - 75,968 = 22,075$

22   Total Problems: Total Correct: Score: © Carson-Dellosa CD-2211

Worksheet 3 (bottom left)

Name _____   Subtracting Large Numbers

Subtract. Then, write the answer in the space provided.

1. $2,375 - 1,194 = 1,181$
2. $6,000 - 1,597 = 4,403$
3. $2,758 - 1,392 = 1,366$
4. $7,594 - 3,283 = 4,311$
5. $62,913 - 41,378 = 21,535$
6. $413,206 - 78,598 = 334,608$
7. $375,211 - 188,456 = 186,755$
8. $754,326 - 561,268 = 193,058$
9. $743,245 - 368,195 = 375,050$
10. $954,328 - 864,597 = 89,731$
11. $880,372 - 751,684 = 128,688$
12. $3,298,174 - 1,367,125 = 1,931,049$
13. $4,369,211 - 2,149,757 = 2,219,454$
14. $7,354,147 - 5,565,402 = 1,788,745$
15. $9,507,366 - 8,237,985 = 1,269,381$

© Carson-Dellosa CD-2211   Total Problems: Total Correct: Score: **23**

Worksheet 4 (bottom right)

Name _____   Estimating Differences

Study the examples below. Round the minuend and subtrahend to the greatest place value. Then, subtract and write the answer in the space provided.

Examples:

576	rounds to	600	476	rounds to	500
− 328	rounds to	− 300	− 123	rounds to	− 100
		300			400

1. $87 \to 90$; $-43 \to -40$; $= 50$
2. $75 \to 80$; $-46 \to -50$; $= 30$
3. $38 \to 40$; $-19 \to -20$; $= 20$
4. $135 \to 100$; $-78 \to -80$; $= 20$
5. $264 \to 300$; $-127 \to -100$; $= 200$
6. $351 \to 400$; $-175 \to -200$; $= 200$
7. $4,286 \to 4,000$; $-2,599 \to -3,000$; $= 1,000$
8. $7,582 \to 8,000$; $-4,378 \to -4,000$; $= 4,000$
9. $9,828 \to 10,000$; $-6,743 \to -7,000$; $= 3,000$
10. $12,622 \to 10,000$; $-9,840 \to -10,000$; $= 0$
11. $17,568 \to 20,000$; $-8,744 \to -9,000$; $= 11,000$
12. $14,727 \to 10,000$; $-9,864 \to -10,000$; $= 0$
13. $75,382 \to 80,000$; $-49,675 \to -50,000$; $= 30,000$
14. $95,460 \to 100,000$; $-74,328 \to -70,000$; $= 30,000$
15. $106,274 \to 100,000$; $-38,591 \to -40,000$; $= 60,000$
16. $116,754 \to 100,000$; $-95,287 \to -100,000$; $= 0$
17. $97,462 \to 100,000$; $-26,561 \to -30,000$; $= 70,000$
18. $174,382 \to 200,000$; $-142,949 \to -100,000$; $= 100,000$

24   Total Problems: Total Correct: Score: © Carson-Dellosa CD-2211

© Carson-Dellosa CD-2211

Worksheet 25 — Subtraction Problem Solving

Name _____   Subtraction Problem Solving

Solve each problem. Show your work and write the answer in the space provided.

1. John had 23 baseball cards. He gave 11 to his friend at school. How many cards does John have left?

$$\begin{array}{r} 23 \\ -11 \\ \hline 12 \text{ cards} \end{array}$$

2. Mr. Faraday's farm has 285 cows. Of the 285, 115 of them are dairy cows. How many of Mr. Faraday's cows are not dairy cows?

$$\begin{array}{r} 285 \\ -115 \\ \hline 170 \text{ cows} \end{array}$$

3. Molly stenciled 96 leaves on the art room's mural. Her teacher decided to cut the mural and remove 29 of the leaves Molly stenciled. How many leaves remain on the mural?

$$\begin{array}{r} 96 \\ -29 \\ \hline 67 \text{ leaves} \end{array}$$

4. Mr. Jackson bought 755 new golf tees. After one month of playing golf, he had lost or broken 294 of them. How many usable golf tees does he have left?

$$\begin{array}{r} 755 \\ -294 \\ \hline 461 \text{ tees} \end{array}$$

5. Jacob and Dominic collected 245 cans for the school can drive. They gave 55 cans to Dominic's little sister for her class to get credit. How many cans does this leave for the boys' class?

$245 - 55 = 190$ cans

6. Mr. Nelson had 346 boxes of merchandise to open and place on shelves at his store. In one day he emptied 284 boxes. How many boxes does he have left to open?

$346 - 284 = 62$ boxes

7. Dan bought 583 square yards of carpet for his basement. He only used 485 square yards. How much carpet did he have left?

$583 - 485 = 98$ square yards

8. Selena has 114 compact discs of music in her collection. If she decides to give away 37 of them, how many will she have left?

$$\begin{array}{r} 114 \\ -37 \\ \hline 77 \text{ compact discs} \end{array}$$

Total Problems: ___   Total Correct: ___   Score: ___   **25**

© Carson-Dellosa CD-2211

Worksheet 26 — Basic Multiplication Facts

Name _____   Basic Multiplication Facts

Multiply. Write the answer on the line provided.

1. $9 \times 6 =$ __54__
2. $7 \times 8 =$ __56__
3. $6 \times 7 =$ __42__
4. $3 \times 8 =$ __24__
5. $3 \times 5 =$ __15__
6. $5 \times 12 =$ __60__
7. $3 \times 4 =$ __12__
8. $8 \times 10 =$ __80__
9. $9 \times 2 =$ __18__
10. $5 \times 4 =$ __20__
11. $4 \times 7 =$ __28__
12. $7 \times 5 =$ __35__
13. $5 \times 5 =$ __25__
14. $2 \times 3 =$ __6__
15. $6 \times 3 =$ __18__
16. $4 \times 4 =$ __16__
17. $8 \times 5 =$ __40__
18. $6 \times 4 =$ __24__
19. $6 \times 5 =$ __30__
20. $3 \times 7 =$ __21__
21. $4 \times 8 =$ __32__
22. $12 \times 6 =$ __72__
23. $7 \times 7 =$ __49__
24. $12 \times 9 =$ __108__
25. $9 \times 5 =$ __45__
26. $7 \times 9 =$ __63__
27. $12 \times 5 =$ __60__
28. $8 \times 2 =$ __16__
29. $5 \times 2 =$ __10__
30. $8 \times 8 =$ __64__
31. $6 \times 6 =$ __36__
32. $7 \times 10 =$ __70__

26   Total Problems: ___   Total Correct: ___   Score: ___   © Carson-Dellosa CD-2211

Worksheet 27 — Mastering Facts

Name _____   Mastering Facts

Study the example below. Find the missing number and write the answer on the line provided.

Example:
$(6 \times \underline{}) \times 2 = 4 \times 3$ $4 \times 3 = 12$, so $(6 \times \underline{}) \times 2 = 12$
$(6 \times \underline{1}) \times 2 = 4 \times 3$

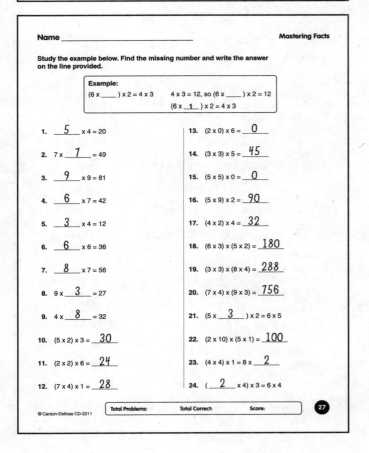

1. $\underline{5} \times 4 = 20$
2. $7 \times \underline{7} = 49$
3. $\underline{9} \times 9 = 81$
4. $\underline{6} \times 7 = 42$
5. $\underline{3} \times 4 = 12$
6. $\underline{6} \times 6 = 36$
7. $\underline{8} \times 7 = 56$
8. $9 \times \underline{3} = 27$
9. $4 \times \underline{8} = 32$
10. $(5 \times 2) \times 3 = \underline{30}$
11. $(2 \times 2) \times 6 = \underline{24}$
12. $(7 \times 4) \times 1 = \underline{28}$
13. $(2 \times 0) \times 6 = \underline{0}$
14. $(3 \times 3) \times 5 = \underline{45}$
15. $(5 \times 5) \times 0 = \underline{0}$
16. $(5 \times 9) \times 2 = \underline{90}$
17. $(4 \times 2) \times 4 = \underline{32}$
18. $(6 \times 3) \times (5 \times 2) = \underline{180}$
19. $(3 \times 3) \times (8 \times 4) = \underline{288}$
20. $(7 \times 4) \times (9 \times 3) = \underline{756}$
21. $(5 \times \underline{3}) \times 2 = 6 \times 5$
22. $(2 \times 10) \times (5 \times 1) = \underline{100}$
23. $(4 \times 4) \times 1 = 8 \times \underline{2}$
24. $(\underline{2} \times 4) \times 3 = 6 \times 4$

Total Problems: ___   Total Correct: ___   Score: ___   **27**

© Carson-Dellosa CD-2211

Worksheet 28 — Multiplying with Zeros

Name _____   Multiplying with Zeros

Multiply. Then, write the answer in the space provided.

1. $\begin{array}{r} 10 \\ \times 5 \\ \hline 50 \end{array}$
2. $\begin{array}{r} 20 \\ \times 4 \\ \hline 80 \end{array}$
3. $\begin{array}{r} 60 \\ \times 8 \\ \hline 480 \end{array}$
4. $\begin{array}{r} 90 \\ \times 2 \\ \hline 180 \end{array}$
5. $\begin{array}{r} 50 \\ \times 5 \\ \hline 250 \end{array}$
6. $\begin{array}{r} 40 \\ \times 3 \\ \hline 120 \end{array}$
7. $\begin{array}{r} 80 \\ \times 5 \\ \hline 400 \end{array}$
8. $\begin{array}{r} 30 \\ \times 7 \\ \hline 210 \end{array}$
9. $\begin{array}{r} 30 \\ \times 12 \\ \hline 360 \end{array}$
10. $\begin{array}{r} 50 \\ \times 25 \\ \hline 1{,}250 \end{array}$
11. $\begin{array}{r} 200 \\ \times 40 \\ \hline 8{,}000 \end{array}$
12. $\begin{array}{r} 800 \\ \times 50 \\ \hline 40{,}000 \end{array}$
13. $\begin{array}{r} 500 \\ \times 30 \\ \hline 15{,}000 \end{array}$
14. $\begin{array}{r} 700 \\ \times 20 \\ \hline 14{,}000 \end{array}$
15. $\begin{array}{r} 400 \\ \times 22 \\ \hline 8{,}800 \end{array}$
16. $\begin{array}{r} 900 \\ \times 60 \\ \hline 54{,}000 \end{array}$
17. $\begin{array}{r} 8{,}000 \\ \times 7 \\ \hline 56{,}000 \end{array}$
18. $\begin{array}{r} 6{,}000 \\ \times 4 \\ \hline 24{,}000 \end{array}$
19. $\begin{array}{r} 5{,}000 \\ \times 200 \\ \hline 1{,}000{,}000 \end{array}$
20. $\begin{array}{r} 3{,}000 \\ \times 600 \\ \hline 1{,}800{,}000 \end{array}$

28   Total Problems: ___   Total Correct: ___   Score: ___   © Carson-Dellosa CD-2211

Panel 1 (page 29)

Name _____ Multiplying One-, Two-, and Three-Digit Numbers

Multiply. Then, write the product in the space provided.

1. 34 × 5 = **170**	6. 294 × 3 = **882**	11. 681 × 33 = **22,473**	16. 560 × 43 = **24,080**
2. 64 × 2 = **128**	7. 38 × 27 = **1,026**	12. 456 × 22 = **10,032**	17. 876 × 43 = **37,668**
3. 58 × 4 = **232**	8. 57 × 16 = **912**	13. 698 × 43 = **30,014**	18. 988 × 73 = **72,124**
4. 145 × 8 = **1,160**	9. 38 × 24 = **912**	14. 246 × 27 = **6,642**	19. 954 × 88 = **83,952**
5. 189 × 9 = **1,701**	10. 75 × 36 = **2,700**	15. 384 × 36 = **13,824**	20. 896 × 57 = **51,072**

Total Problems: ___ Total Correct: ___ Score: ___ **29**

© Carson-Dellosa CD-2211

Panel 2 (page 30)

Name _____ Estimating Products

Study the examples below. Estimate and write the answer in the space provided.

Examples:

35 rounds to 40	560 rounds to 600
× 15 rounds to × 20	× 435 rounds to × 400
800	**240,400**

1. 28 × 12 → 30 × 10 = **300**	5. 75 × 44 → 80 × 40 = **3,200**	9. 1,495 × 287 → 1,000 × 300 = **300,000**	13. 7,852 × 572 → 8,000 × 600 = **4,800,000**
2. 32 × 19 → 30 × 20 = **600**	6. 182 × 106 → 200 × 100 = **20,000**	10. 2,362 × 488 → 2,000 × 500 = **1,000,000**	14. 9,338 × 623 → 9,000 × 600 = **5,400,000**
3. 43 × 56 → 40 × 60 = **2,400**	7. 257 × 218 → 300 × 200 = **60,000**	11. 3,825 × 464 → 4,000 × 500 = **2,000,000**	15. 6,515 × 321 → 7,000 × 300 = **2,100,000**
4. 64 × 39 → 60 × 40 = **2,400**	8. 378 × 217 → 400 × 200 = **80,000**	12. 5,673 × 2,587 → 6,000 × 3,000 = **18,000,000**	16. 7,595 × 752 → 8,000 × 800 = **6,400,000**

30 Total Problems: ___ Total Correct: ___ Score: ___

© Carson-Dellosa CD-2211

Panel 3 (page 31)

Name _____ Estimating Products

Estimate. Write the answer in the space provided.

1. 16 × 12 → 20 × 10 = **200**	5. 354 × 24 → 400 × 20 = **8,000**	9. 2,995 × 157 → 3,000 × 200 = **600,000**	13. 9,761 × 648 → 10,000 × 600 = **6,000,000**
2. 45 × 19 → 50 × 20 = **1,000**	6. 781 × 60 → 800 × 60 = **48,000**	10. 5,247 × 323 → 5,000 × 300 = **1,500,000**	14. 10,528 × 1,333 → 10,000 × 1,000 = **10,000,000**
3. 66 × 17 → 70 × 20 = **1,400**	7. 547 × 58 → 500 × 60 = **30,000**	11. 8,655 × 124 → 9,000 × 100 = **900,000**	15. 8,495 × 126 → 8,000 × 100 = **800,000**
4. 79 × 47 → 80 × 50 = **4,000**	8. 547 × 25 → 500 × 30 = **15,000**	12. 8,473 × 1,560 → 8,000 × 2,000 = **16,000,000**	16. 6,305 × 172 → 6,000 × 200 = **1,200,000**

Total Problems: ___ Total Correct: ___ Score: ___ **31**

© Carson-Dellosa CD-2211

Panel 4 (page 32)

Name _____ Multiplication Practice

Multiply. Write the answer in the space provided.

1. 29 × 41 = **1,189**	6. 36 × 25 = **900**	11. 167 × 32 = **5,344**	16. 654 × 86 = **56,244**
2. 60 × 32 = **1,920**	7. 94 × 33 = **3,102**	12. 243 × 81 = **19,683**	17. 743 × 39 = **28,977**
3. 45 × 26 = **1,170**	8. 86 × 41 = **3,526**	13. 362 × 31 = **11,222**	18. 894 × 27 = **24,138**
4. 73 × 42 = **3,066**	9. 72 × 51 = **3,672**	14. 425 × 64 = **27,200**	19. 635 × 43 = **27,305**
5. 52 × 37 = **1,924**	10. 98 × 45 = **4,410**	15. 536 × 92 = **49,312**	20. 862 × 68 = **58,616**

32 Total Problems: ___ Total Correct: ___ Score: ___

© Carson-Dellosa CD-2211

© Carson-Dellosa CD-2211

Multiplication Practice

Multiply. Write the answer in the space provided.

1. 352 × 28 = 9,856	5. 863 × 74 = 63,862	9. 2,368 × 127 = 300,736	13. 2,206 × 700 = 1,544,200
2. 525 × 64 = 33,600	6. 909 × 83 = 75,447	10. 4,987 × 521 = 2,598,227	14. 6,843 × 811 = 5,549,673
3. 791 × 37 = 29,267	7. 1,042 × 68 = 70,856	11. 3,647 × 86 = 313,642	15. 5,206 × 1,673 = 8,709,638
4. 644 × 92 = 59,248	8. 1,837 × 55 = 101,035	12. 8,172 × 348 = 2,843,856	16. 4,137 × 3,275 = 13,548,675

Total Problems: Total Correct: Score: 33

© Carson-Dellosa CD-2211

Multiplication Problem Solving

Solve each word problem. Show your work and write the answer in the space provided.

1. Melanie bought 7 packages of greeting cards. Each package had 9 cards inside. How many greeting cards did she get in all?
7 x 9 = 63 cards

2. Grace saw 16 cages of birds at the zoo's aviary. The sign said each cage had 12 birds. How many birds were in the aviary cages in all?
16 x 12 = 192 birds

3. Matthew unpacked 43 boxes of lightbulbs for the discount warehouse. Each box contained 6 bulbs. How many bulbs were there in all 43 boxes?
43 x 6 = 258 bulbs

4. Nell sold 125 packages of cookies at the bake sale. Each package was tied with 2 ribbons. How many ribbons were used in all?
125 x 2 = 250 ribbons

5. Mr. Harding gave out 15 coupons per hour at the appliance show. After 2 days at the show, working 14 hours total, how many coupons did he distribute?
15 x 14 = 210 coupons

6. Chris walked 4 miles a day for 21 days. How many miles did she walk in all?
4 x 21 = 84 miles

7. Kelly practiced her flute 30 minutes a day for 15 days. After the 15 days were completed, how many minutes had she practiced?
30 x 15 = 450 minutes

8. LaToya played her new CD for 3 hours every day the first 5 days she had it. How many hours did she play the CD? How many minutes was this?
3 x 5 = 15 hours
15 x 60 = 900 minutes

34 Total Problems: Total Correct: Score: © Carson-Dellosa CD-2211

Division Basic Facts

Divide. Write the answer on the line provided.

1. 9 ÷ 3 = 3
2. 24 ÷ 4 = 6
3. 49 ÷ 7 = 7
4. 32 ÷ 8 = 4
5. 25 ÷ 5 = 5
6. 16 ÷ 8 = 2
7. 35 ÷ 7 = 5
8. 20 ÷ 5 = 4
9. 12 ÷ 4 = 3
10. 15 ÷ 3 = 5
11. 24 ÷ 3 = 8
12. 36 ÷ 6 = 6
13. 60 ÷ 5 = 12
14. 18 ÷ 6 = 3
15. 80 ÷ 8 = 10
16. 18 ÷ 2 = 9
17. 40 ÷ 8 = 5
18. 108 ÷ 9 = 12
19. 30 ÷ 6 = 5
20. 45 ÷ 9 = 5
21. 42 ÷ 6 = 7
22. 28 ÷ 7 = 4
23. 63 ÷ 7 = 9
24. 90 ÷ 9 = 10
25. 56 ÷ 8 = 7
26. 21 ÷ 7 = 3
27. 16 ÷ 8 = 2
28. 6 ÷ 0 = 0
29. 54 ÷ 6 = 9
30. 64 ÷ 8 = 8
31. 10 ÷ 2 = 5
32. 21 ÷ 3 = 7

Total Problems: Total Correct: Score: 35
© Carson-Dellosa CD-2211

Division Facts 0–1

Study the box below. Divide and write the quotient in the space provided.

Rules: When a number is divided by 1, the quotient is the same as the number. When a number is divided by 0, the quotient is 0.
Examples: 1)5 = 5   0)15 = 0

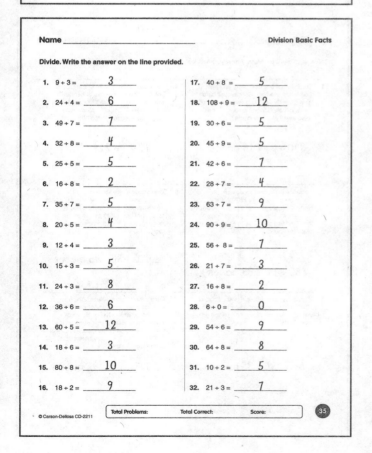

1. 1)7 = 7
2. 0)6 = 0
3. 1)8 = 8
4. 1)9 = 9
5. 1)3 = 3
6. 0)5 = 0
7. 0)2 = 0
8. 1)4 = 4
9. 1)2 = 2
10. 1)13 = 13
11. 0)25 = 0
12. 1)17 = 17
13. 1)12 = 12
14. 1)47 = 47
15. 0)28 = 0
16. 0)20 = 0
17. 1)79 = 79
18. 1)84 = 84
19. 0)76 = 0
20. 0)96 = 0

36 Total Problems: Total Correct: Score: © Carson-Dellosa CD-2211

© Carson-Dellosa CD-2211

85

Worksheet 37

Name _____   Division Facts 8–9

Study the box below. Divide and write the quotient in the space provided.

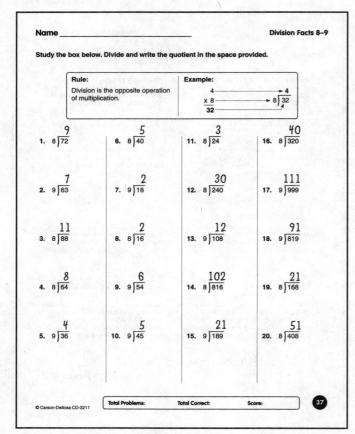

Rule:
Division is the opposite operation of multiplication.

Example:

$$
\begin{array}{r}
4 \\
\times\ 8 \\
\hline
32
\end{array}
\quad\longrightarrow\quad
8\,\overline{)\,32}\ =\ 4
$$

1. $8\overline{)72}$ = **9**
6. $8\overline{)40}$ = **5**
11. $8\overline{)24}$ = **3**
16. $8\overline{)320}$ = **40**

2. $9\overline{)63}$ = **7**
7. $9\overline{)18}$ = **2**
12. $8\overline{)240}$ = **30**
17. $9\overline{)999}$ = **111**

3. $8\overline{)88}$ = **11**
8. $8\overline{)16}$ = **2**
13. $9\overline{)108}$ = **12**
18. $9\overline{)819}$ = **91**

4. $8\overline{)64}$ = **8**
9. $9\overline{)54}$ = **6**
14. $8\overline{)816}$ = **102**
19. $8\overline{)168}$ = **21**

5. $9\overline{)36}$ = **4**
10. $9\overline{)45}$ = **5**
15. $9\overline{)189}$ = **21**
20. $8\overline{)408}$ = **51**

Total Problems: _____   Total Correct: _____   Score: _____   **37**

© Carson-Dellosa CD-2211

Worksheet 38

Name _____   Division with Two-Digit Divisors

Study the examples below. Divide and write the answer in the space provided.

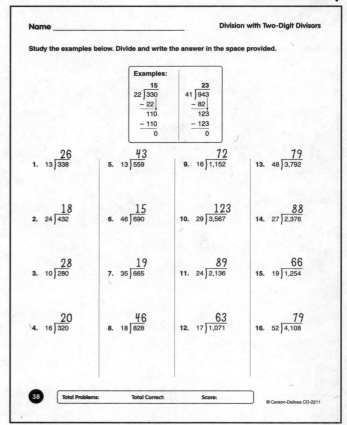

Examples:

$$
\begin{array}{r}
15 \\
22\,\overline{)330} \\
-22 \\
\hline
110 \\
-110 \\
\hline
0
\end{array}
\qquad
\begin{array}{r}
23 \\
41\,\overline{)943} \\
-82 \\
\hline
123 \\
-123 \\
\hline
0
\end{array}
$$

1. $13\overline{)338}$ = **26**
5. $13\overline{)559}$ = **43**
9. $16\overline{)1,152}$ = **72**
13. $48\overline{)3,792}$ = **79**

2. $24\overline{)432}$ = **18**
6. $46\overline{)690}$ = **15**
10. $29\overline{)3,567}$ = **123**
14. $27\overline{)2,376}$ = **88**

3. $10\overline{)280}$ = **28**
7. $35\overline{)665}$ = **19**
11. $24\overline{)2,136}$ = **89**
15. $19\overline{)1,254}$ = **66**

4. $16\overline{)320}$ = **20**
8. $18\overline{)828}$ = **46**
12. $17\overline{)1,071}$ = **63**
16. $52\overline{)4,108}$ = **79**

38   Total Problems: _____   Total Correct: _____   Score: _____

© Carson-Dellosa CD-2211

Worksheet 39

Name _____   Division with Five-Digit Dividends

Divide, then write the answer in the space provided.

1. $46\overline{)19,550}$ = **425**
4. $32\overline{)75,040}$ = **2,345**
7. $84\overline{)19,824}$ = **236**
10. $24\overline{)27,624}$ = **1,151**

2. $71\overline{)24,850}$ = **350**
5. $56\overline{)23,520}$ = **420**
8. $62\overline{)22,444}$ = **362**
11. $45\overline{)43,335}$ = **963**

3. $25\overline{)31,375}$ = **1,255**
6. $40\overline{)30,000}$ = **750**
9. $89\overline{)56,070}$ = **630**
12. $18\overline{)62,298}$ = **3,461**

Total Problems: _____   Total Correct: _____   Score: _____   **39**

© Carson-Dellosa CD-2211

Worksheet 40

Name _____   Division Problem Solving

Solve each word problem. Show your work and write the answer in the space provided.

1. Travis had a birthday party and invited 26 friends. He had 390 baseball cards to give as party favors. How many baseball cards did each friend receive if Travis gave away all of his cards?

$390 \div 26 = 15$ cards

2. Terrance is reading a book about computers. There are 882 pages in the book. Terrance wants to finish the book in 2 weeks. How many pages does he need to read each day to finish the book within his deadline?

$2 \times 7 = 14$ days
$882 \div 14 = 63$ pages

3. Susan has 560 different horse figures. She has 16 shelves on which to place her figures. How many horses will go on each shelf?

$560 \div 16 = 35$ horses

4. Gail needed more room in her closet. She decided to take half of her outfits and place them in the attic closet. She had a total of 42 outfits. How many outfits were moved to the attic?

$42 \div 2 = 21$ outfits

5. Jason went to the store to buy candy for his classmates. There are 36 students in his homeroom. He bought a bag of candy that has 1,620 pieces inside. How many pieces will each classmate receive?

$1,620 \div 36 = 45$ pieces

6. Anna's fourth grade class is planning a field trip to an amusement park. There are 29 students in her class. Each student must earn points to go on the trip. All 29 students must earn a total of 2,697 points. How many points must each student earn?

$2,697 \div 29 = 93$ points

40   Total Problems: _____   Total Correct: _____   Score: _____

© Carson-Dellosa CD-2211

© Carson-Dellosa CD-2211

Worksheet 41

Name _____ **Division with and without Remainders**

Study the box below. Divide each problem, making sure the remainder is less than the divisor. Then, write the answer in the space provided.

Rules:
1. Follow the steps of long division.
2. Compare the difference with the divisor. If it is larger, take more groups out of the dividend. If it is smaller, the number is the remainder.

Example:
```
    33 R3
  4)135
   -12
    15
   -12
     3
```
(R = remainder)

1. 8)489 = **61 R1**
4. 6)576 = **96**
7. 8)6,312 = **789**
10. 7)2,537 = **362 R3**

2. 5)921 = **184 R1**
5. 7)234 = **33 R3**
8. 9)8,329 = **925 R4**
11. 8)1,778 = **222 R2**

3. 2)835 = **417 R1**
6. 6)379 = **63 R1**
9. 5)3,400 = **680**
12. 7)1,652 = **236**

© Carson-Dellosa CD-2211   Total Problems: ___ Total Correct: ___ Score: ___   **41**

Worksheet 42

Name _____ **Estimating Quotients**

Study the example below. Estimate the quotients. Then, write the answer on the line provided.

Example:
116 ÷ 4 = → 120 ÷ 4 = → 120 ÷ 4 = **30**
Round the dividend. 116 rounds to 120. Use mental math to divide.

1. 631 ÷ 3 = **630 ÷ 3 = 210**
2. 224 ÷ 4 = **240 ÷ 4 = 60**
3. 654 ÷ 5 = **650 ÷ 5 = 130**
4. 486 ÷ 7 = **490 ÷ 7 = 70**
5. 709 ÷ 9 = **720 ÷ 9 = 80**
6. 386 ÷ 3 = **390 ÷ 3 = 130**
7. 427 ÷ 5 = **450 ÷ 5 = 90**
8. 283 ÷ 7 = **280 ÷ 7 = 40**
9. 162 ÷ 8 = **160 ÷ 8 = 20**
10. 628 ÷ 9 = **630 ÷ 9 = 70**
11. 438 ÷ 2 = **440 ÷ 2 = 220**
12. 981 ÷ 4 = **1,000 ÷ 4 = 250**

13. 656 ÷ 2 = **660 ÷ 2 = 330**
14. 684 ÷ 4 = **680 ÷ 4 = 170**
15. 864 ÷ 4 = **860 ÷ 4 = 215**
16. 788 ÷ 5 = **800 ÷ 5 = 160**
17. 841 ÷ 7 = **840 ÷ 7 = 120**
18. 423 ÷ 2 = **420 ÷ 2 = 210**
19. 869 ÷ 5 = **870 ÷ 5 = 174**
20. 648 ÷ 5 = **650 ÷ 5 = 130**
21. 903 ÷ 3 = **900 ÷ 3 = 300**
22. 769 ÷ 7 = **770 ÷ 7 = 110**
23. 945 ÷ 5 = **950 ÷ 5 = 190**
24. 751 ÷ 6 = **780 ÷ 6 = 130**

42   Total Problems: ___ Total Correct: ___ Score: ___   © Carson-Dellosa CD-2211

Worksheet 43

Name _____ **Division Practice**

Divide. Write the quotient in the space provided.

1. 6)604 = **100 R4**
5. 6)788 = **131 R2**
9. 39)400 = **10 R10**
13. 5)4,672 = **934 R2**

2. 5)716 = **143 R1**
6. 4)791 = **197 R3**
10. 57)665 = **11 R38**
14. 7)4,347 = **621**

3. 8)819 = **102 R3**
7. 8)977 = **122 R1**
11. 47)549 = **11 R32**
15. 8)5,789 = **723 R5**

4. 3)901 = **300 R1**
8. 3)987 = **329**
12. 27)344 = **12 R20**
16. 8)63,456 = **7,932**

© Carson-Dellosa CD-2211   Total Problems: ___ Total Correct: ___ Score: ___   **43**

Worksheet 44

Name _____ **Division Problem Solving**

Solve each word problem. Show your work and write the answer in the space provided.

1. Bruce earned $650.00 for delivering newspapers. He earned his money over 5 weeks. How much did he earn each week?

   $650.00 ÷ 5 = $130.00

2. Barbara wanted to knit 8 sweaters for each of her grandchildren. If Barbara knitted 120 sweaters during the entire year, how many grandchildren does Barbara have?

   120 ÷ 8 = 15 grandchildren

3. Kameelah got a box of building blocks. The box had 789 blocks inside. If Kameelah made 3 towers with an equal amount of blocks, how many blocks were used to build each tower?

   789 ÷ 3 = 263 blocks

4. Susan goes to the gym every day. She wants to burn calories during her workout. She needs to burn 300 calories every hour. How many calories does Susan need to burn per minute?

   300 ÷ 60 = 5 calories per minute

5. Fred has 24 friends that are coming to his Fourth of July party. He buys 144 cans of soda. How many cans of soda can each guest have?

   144 ÷ 24 = 6 cans of soda

6. Owners from 11 different music companies have been invited to a music festival. Each owner brings a number of compact discs to the festival. If there were a total of 6,215 compact discs and each owner brought the same amount, how many compact discs did each owner bring?

   6,215 ÷ 11 = 565 compact discs

44   Total Problems: ___ Total Correct: ___ Score: ___   © Carson-Dellosa CD-2211

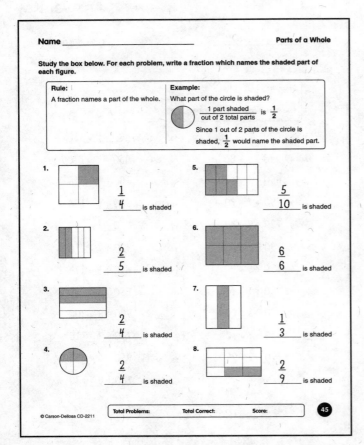

Name _____ Parts of a Whole

Study the box below. For each problem, write a fraction which names the shaded part of each figure.

Rule:	Example:
A fraction names a part of the whole.	What part of the circle is shaded? $\frac{1 \text{ part shaded}}{\text{out of 2 total parts}}$ is $\frac{1}{2}$. Since 1 out of 2 parts of the circle is shaded, $\frac{1}{2}$ would name the shaded part.

1. $\frac{1}{4}$ is shaded

2. $\frac{2}{5}$ is shaded

3. $\frac{2}{4}$ is shaded

4. $\frac{2}{4}$ is shaded

5. $\frac{5}{10}$ is shaded

6. $\frac{6}{6}$ is shaded

7. $\frac{1}{3}$ is shaded

8. $\frac{2}{9}$ is shaded

© Carson-Dellosa CD-2211

Total Problems: ___ Total Correct: ___ Score: ___ 45

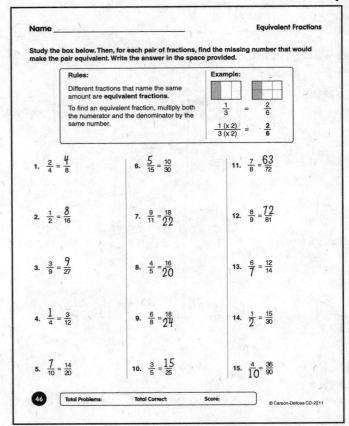

Name _____ Equivalent Fractions

Study the box below. Then, for each pair of fractions, find the missing number that would make the pair equivalent. Write the answer in the space provided.

Rules:	Example:
Different fractions that name the same amount are **equivalent fractions**. To find an equivalent fraction, multiply both the numerator and the denominator by the same number.	$\frac{1}{3} = \frac{2}{6}$ $\frac{1 (x 2)}{3 (x 2)} = \frac{2}{6}$

46

1. $\frac{2}{4} = \frac{4}{8}$

2. $\frac{1}{2} = \frac{8}{16}$

3. $\frac{3}{9} = \frac{9}{27}$

4. $\frac{1}{4} = \frac{3}{12}$

5. $\frac{7}{10} = \frac{14}{20}$

6. $\frac{5}{15} = \frac{10}{30}$

7. $\frac{9}{11} = \frac{18}{22}$

8. $\frac{4}{5} = \frac{16}{20}$

9. $\frac{6}{8} = \frac{18}{24}$

10. $\frac{3}{5} = \frac{15}{25}$

11. $\frac{7}{8} = \frac{63}{72}$

12. $\frac{8}{9} = \frac{72}{81}$

13. $\frac{6}{7} = \frac{12}{14}$

14. $\frac{1}{2} = \frac{15}{30}$

15. $\frac{4}{10} = \frac{36}{90}$

Total Problems: ___ Total Correct: ___ Score: ___ © Carson-Dellosa CD-2211

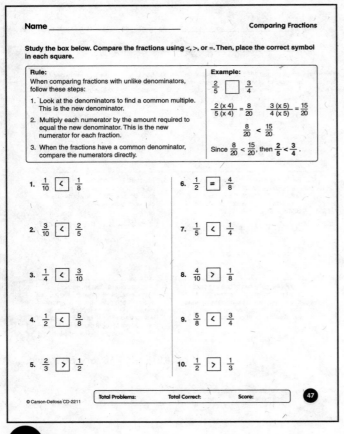

Name _____ Comparing Fractions

Study the box below. Compare the fractions using <, >, or =. Then, place the correct symbol in each square.

Rule:	Example:
When comparing fractions with unlike denominators, follow these steps: 1. Look at the denominators to find a common multiple. This is the new denominator. 2. Multiply each numerator by the amount required to equal the new denominator. This is the new numerator for each fraction. 3. When the fractions have a common denominator, compare the numerators directly.	$\frac{2}{5} \square \frac{3}{4}$ $\frac{2 (x 4)}{5 (x 4)} = \frac{8}{20}$ $\frac{3 (x 5)}{4 (x 5)} = \frac{15}{20}$ $\frac{8}{20} < \frac{15}{20}$ Since $\frac{8}{20} < \frac{15}{20}$, then $\frac{2}{5} < \frac{3}{4}$.

1. $\frac{1}{10}$ < $\frac{1}{8}$

2. $\frac{3}{10}$ < $\frac{2}{5}$

3. $\frac{1}{4}$ < $\frac{3}{10}$

4. $\frac{1}{2}$ < $\frac{5}{8}$

5. $\frac{2}{3}$ > $\frac{1}{2}$

6. $\frac{1}{2}$ = $\frac{4}{8}$

7. $\frac{1}{5}$ < $\frac{1}{4}$

8. $\frac{4}{10}$ > $\frac{1}{8}$

9. $\frac{5}{8}$ < $\frac{3}{4}$

10. $\frac{1}{2}$ > $\frac{1}{3}$

© Carson-Dellosa CD-2211

Total Problems: ___ Total Correct: ___ Score: ___ 47

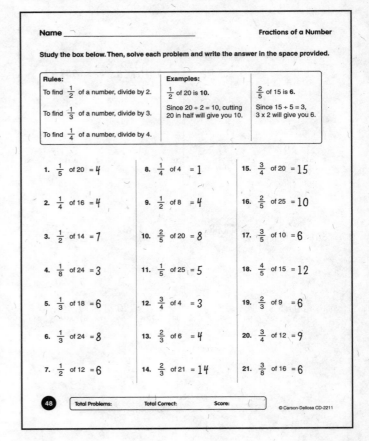

Name _____ Fractions of a Number

Study the box below. Then, solve each problem and write the answer in the space provided.

Rules:	Examples:	
To find $\frac{1}{2}$ of a number, divide by 2.	$\frac{1}{2}$ of 20 is **10**.	$\frac{2}{5}$ of 15 is **6**.
To find $\frac{1}{3}$ of a number, divide by 3.	Since 20 ÷ 2 = 10, cutting 20 in half will give you 10.	Since 15 ÷ 5 = 3, 3 x 2 will give you 6.
To find $\frac{1}{4}$ of a number, divide by 4.		

48

1. $\frac{1}{5}$ of 20 = 4

2. $\frac{1}{4}$ of 16 = 4

3. $\frac{1}{2}$ of 14 = 7

4. $\frac{1}{8}$ of 24 = 3

5. $\frac{1}{3}$ of 18 = 6

6. $\frac{1}{3}$ of 24 = 8

7. $\frac{1}{2}$ of 12 = 6

8. $\frac{1}{4}$ of 4 = 1

9. $\frac{1}{2}$ of 8 = 4

10. $\frac{2}{5}$ of 20 = 8

11. $\frac{1}{5}$ of 25 = 5

12. $\frac{3}{4}$ of 4 = 3

13. $\frac{2}{3}$ of 6 = 4

14. $\frac{2}{3}$ of 21 = 14

15. $\frac{3}{4}$ of 20 = 15

16. $\frac{2}{5}$ of 25 = 10

17. $\frac{3}{5}$ of 10 = 6

18. $\frac{4}{5}$ of 15 = 12

19. $\frac{2}{3}$ of 9 = 6

20. $\frac{3}{4}$ of 12 = 9

21. $\frac{3}{8}$ of 16 = 6

Total Problems: ___ Total Correct: ___ Score: ___ © Carson-Dellosa CD-2211

Page 49 — Adding and Subtracting Like Denominators

Name _____

Study the box below. Then, solve each problem, paying careful attention to the sign. Write the answer in the space provided.

Rule:
When adding or subtracting fractions with the same denominator:
1. Add or subtract their numerators.
2. Write that number over the same denominator.

Examples:
$$\frac{2}{10} + \frac{4}{10} = \frac{6}{10}$$
$$\frac{9}{10} - \frac{3}{10} = \frac{6}{10}$$

1. $\frac{2}{6} - \frac{1}{6} = \frac{1}{6}$

2. $\frac{1}{4} + \frac{1}{4} = \frac{2}{4} \text{ or } \frac{1}{2}$

3. $\frac{4}{6} - \frac{2}{6} = \frac{2}{6}$

4. $\frac{2}{4} + \frac{1}{4} = \frac{3}{4}$

5. $\frac{1}{10} + \frac{5}{10} = \frac{6}{10}$

6. $\frac{9}{10} - \frac{4}{10} = \frac{5}{10} \text{ or } \frac{1}{2}$

7. $\frac{1}{6} + \frac{4}{6} = \frac{5}{6}$

8. $\frac{7}{8} - \frac{1}{8} = \frac{6}{8}$ $\frac{6}{8}$

9. $\frac{3}{12} + \frac{4}{12} = \frac{7}{12}$

10. $\frac{9}{8} - \frac{2}{8} = \frac{7}{8}$

11. $\frac{2}{10} - \frac{1}{10} = \frac{1}{10}$

12. $\frac{1}{10} + \frac{8}{10} = \frac{9}{10}$

13. $\frac{15}{18} - \frac{8}{18} = \frac{7}{18}$

14. $\frac{4}{8} + \frac{3}{8} = \frac{7}{8}$

15. $\frac{8}{10} - \frac{5}{10} = \frac{3}{10}$

16. $\frac{3}{6} + \frac{2}{6} = \frac{5}{6}$

17. $\frac{8}{8} - \frac{2}{8} = \frac{6}{8}$

18. $\frac{2}{16} + \frac{9}{16} = \frac{11}{16}$

© Carson-Dellosa CD-2211   Total Problems: ____ Total Correct: ____ Score: ____   **49**

Page 50 — Adding and Subtracting Unlike Denominators

Name _____

Study the box below. Then, use equivalent fractions to find the sums or differences of the following problems. Write the answer in the space provided.

Rule:
When adding or subtracting fractions with different denominators:
1. Look at the denominators.
2. Find the equivalent fractions.
3. Add or subtract the new fractions.
4. If necessary, convert the fraction to a mixed number.

Examples:

$\frac{2}{4} (\times 2) = \frac{4}{8}$
$+ \frac{5}{8} (\times 1) = \frac{5}{8}$
$\frac{9}{8} = 1\frac{1}{8}$

$\frac{3}{5} (\times 2) = \frac{6}{10}$
$- \frac{1}{10} (\times 1) = \frac{1}{10}$
$\frac{5}{10} = \frac{1}{2}$

1. $\frac{3}{8} = \frac{3}{8}$
$+ \frac{3}{4} = \frac{6}{8}$
$1\frac{1}{8}$

2. $\frac{7}{8} = \frac{7}{8}$
$- \frac{1}{2} = \frac{4}{8}$
$\frac{3}{8}$

3. $\frac{1}{4} = \frac{2}{8}$
$+ \frac{3}{8} = \frac{3}{8}$
$\frac{5}{8}$

4. $\frac{5}{8} = \frac{5}{8}$
$- \frac{1}{4} = \frac{2}{8}$
$\frac{3}{8}$

5. $\frac{3}{10} = \frac{3}{10}$
$+ \frac{1}{5} = \frac{2}{10}$
$\frac{5}{10} \text{ or } \frac{1}{2}$

6. $\frac{5}{6} = \frac{5}{6}$
$- \frac{1}{3} = \frac{2}{6}$
$\frac{3}{6} \text{ or } \frac{1}{2}$

7. $\frac{2}{5} = \frac{4}{10}$
$+ \frac{1}{10} = \frac{1}{10}$
$\frac{5}{10} \text{ or } \frac{1}{2}$

8. $\frac{5}{8} = \frac{5}{8}$
$- \frac{1}{2} = \frac{4}{8}$
$\frac{1}{8}$

9. $\frac{3}{4} = \frac{3}{4}$
$+ \frac{1}{2} = \frac{2}{4}$
$1\frac{1}{4}$

50   Total Problems: ____ Total Correct: ____ Score: ____   © Carson-Dellosa CD-2211

Page 51 — Multiplying Single Fractions

Name _____

Study the box below. Multiply each problem and write the answer in the space provided.

Rule:
1. Multiply the numerators.
2. Multiply the denominators.
3. Write the new fraction.

Example:
$$\frac{2}{3} \times \frac{3}{4} = \frac{6}{12}$$

1. $\frac{5}{6} \times \frac{1}{4} = \frac{5}{24}$

2. $\frac{1}{4} \times \frac{1}{8} = \frac{1}{32}$

3. $\frac{1}{9} \times \frac{1}{9} = \frac{1}{81}$

4. $\frac{5}{8} \times \frac{3}{4} = \frac{15}{32}$

5. $\frac{5}{9} \times \frac{2}{3} = \frac{10}{27}$

6. $\frac{3}{4} \times \frac{3}{4} = \frac{9}{16}$

7. $\frac{7}{8} \times \frac{5}{6} = \frac{35}{48}$

8. $\frac{3}{8} \times \frac{2}{5} = \frac{6}{40}$

9. $\frac{5}{6} \times \frac{1}{6} = \frac{5}{36}$

10. $\frac{2}{3} \times \frac{1}{3} = \frac{2}{9}$

11. $\frac{6}{7} \times \frac{1}{4} = \frac{6}{28}$

12. $\frac{5}{12} \times \frac{5}{8} = \frac{25}{96}$

13. $\frac{2}{3} \times \frac{11}{12} = \frac{22}{36}$

14. $\frac{3}{5} \times \frac{8}{9} = \frac{24}{45}$

15. $\frac{6}{10} \times \frac{1}{3} = \frac{6}{30}$

16. $\frac{6}{8} \times \frac{4}{8} = \frac{24}{64}$

17. $\frac{5}{7} \times \frac{4}{9} = \frac{20}{63}$

18. $\frac{2}{4} \times \frac{2}{5} = \frac{4}{20}$

© Carson-Dellosa CD-2211   Total Problems: ____ Total Correct: ____ Score: ____   **51**

Page 52 — Mixed Numbers

Name _____

Study the box below. Write a mixed number for each fraction. Write the answer in the space provided.

Rule:
1. Divide the numerator by the denominator.
2. Write the quotient as the whole number.
3. The remainder is written as the numerator over the denominator (divisor).

Example:
$$\frac{19}{3} \rightarrow 3\overline{)19} \begin{array}{c} 6 \text{ R}1 \\ -18 \\ \hline 1 \end{array} \quad 6\frac{1}{3}$$

1. $\frac{37}{5} = 7\frac{2}{5}$

2. $\frac{17}{2} = 8\frac{1}{2}$

3. $\frac{11}{4} = 2\frac{3}{4}$

4. $\frac{27}{4} = 6\frac{3}{4}$

5. $\frac{11}{3} = 3\frac{2}{3}$

6. $\frac{35}{4} = 8\frac{3}{4}$

7. $\frac{15}{4} = 3\frac{3}{4}$

8. $\frac{19}{6} = 3\frac{1}{6}$

9. $\frac{29}{3} = 9\frac{2}{3}$

10. $\frac{23}{6} = 3\frac{5}{6}$

11. $\frac{19}{2} = 9\frac{1}{2}$

12. $\frac{9}{4} = 2\frac{1}{4}$

13. $\frac{71}{8} = 8\frac{7}{8}$

14. $\frac{36}{5} = 7\frac{1}{5}$

15. $\frac{39}{7} = 5\frac{4}{7}$

16. $\frac{13}{2} = 6\frac{1}{2}$

17. $\frac{22}{3} = 7\frac{1}{3}$

18. $\frac{15}{6} = 2\frac{3}{6} \text{ or } 2\frac{1}{2}$

52   Total Problems: ____ Total Correct: ____ Score: ____   © Carson-Dellosa CD-2211

Worksheet 53 — Improper Fractions

Name _____   Improper Fractions

Study the box below. Write an improper fraction for each mixed number. Write the answer in the space provided.

Rule:
1. Multiple the denominator and the whole number.
2. Add the numerator to the product.
3. Place the answer over the denominator.

Example:

$4\frac{3}{4}$

$4 \times 4 = 16 \longrightarrow 16 + 3 = 19 \longrightarrow \frac{19}{4}$

1. $2\frac{3}{4} = \frac{11}{4}$

2. $6\frac{4}{7} = \frac{46}{7}$

3. $4\frac{5}{6} = \frac{29}{6}$

4. $8\frac{2}{4} = \frac{34}{4}$

5. $10\frac{4}{8} = \frac{84}{8}$

6. $7\frac{2}{5} = \frac{37}{5}$

7. $3\frac{5}{8} = \frac{29}{8}$

8. $9\frac{3}{9} = \frac{84}{9}$

9. $4\frac{2}{3} = \frac{14}{3}$

10. $5\frac{1}{5} = \frac{26}{5}$

11. $1\frac{3}{4} = \frac{7}{4}$

12. $2\frac{3}{8} = \frac{19}{8}$

13. $6\frac{7}{9} = \frac{61}{9}$

14. $3\frac{2}{5} = \frac{17}{5}$

15. $5\frac{2}{7} = \frac{37}{7}$

16. $4\frac{1}{2} = \frac{9}{2}$

17. $7\frac{3}{4} = \frac{31}{4}$

18. $1\frac{7}{8} = \frac{15}{8}$

Total Problems: Total Correct: Score: 53

© Carson-Dellosa CD-2211

Worksheet 54 — Fraction Problem Solving

Name _____   Fraction Problem Solving

Solve each word problem. Show your work and write the answer in the space provided.

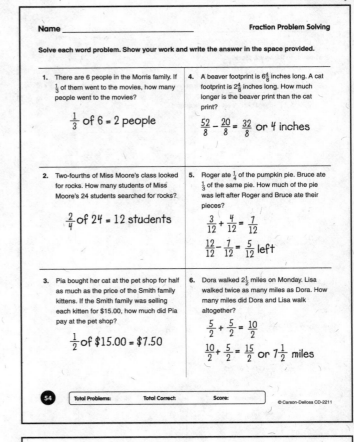

1. There are 6 people in the Morris family. If $\frac{1}{3}$ of them went to the movies, how many people went to the movies?

$\frac{1}{3}$ of 6 = 2 people

2. Two-fourths of Miss Moore's class looked for rocks. How many students of Miss Moore's 24 students searched for rocks?

$\frac{2}{4}$ of 24 = 12 students

3. Pia bought her cat at the pet shop for half as much as the price of the Smith family kittens. If the Smith family was selling each kitten for $15.00, how much did Pia pay at the pet shop?

$\frac{1}{2}$ of $15.00 = $7.50

4. A beaver footprint is $6\frac{4}{8}$ inches long. A cat footprint is $2\frac{4}{8}$ inches long. How much longer is the beaver print than the cat print?

$\frac{52}{8} - \frac{20}{8} = \frac{32}{8}$ or 4 inches

5. Roger ate $\frac{1}{4}$ of the pumpkin pie. Bruce ate $\frac{1}{3}$ of the same pie. How much of the pie was left after Roger and Bruce ate their pieces?

$\frac{3}{12} + \frac{4}{12} = \frac{7}{12}$

$\frac{12}{12} - \frac{7}{12} = \frac{5}{12}$ left

6. Dora walked $2\frac{1}{2}$ miles on Monday. Lisa walked twice as many miles as Dora. How many miles did Dora and Lisa walk altogether?

$\frac{5}{2} + \frac{5}{2} = \frac{10}{2}$

$\frac{10}{2} + \frac{5}{2} = \frac{15}{2}$ or $7\frac{1}{2}$ miles

54   Total Problems: Total Correct: Score: © Carson-Dellosa CD-2211

Worksheet 55 — Place Value

Name _____   Place Value

Study the examples below. Then, write the decimal for each problem in the space provided.

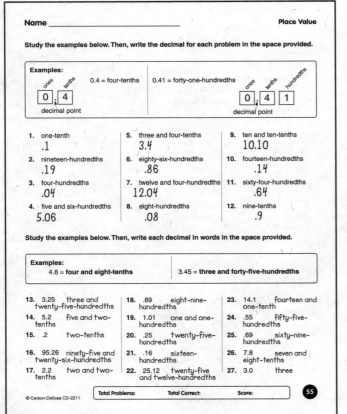

Examples:

ones	tenths
0	4

decimal point

0.4 = four-tenths   0.41 = forty-one-hundredths

ones	tenths	hundredths
0	4	1

decimal point

1. one-tenth   .1
2. nineteen-hundredths   .19
3. four-hundredths   .04
4. five and six-hundredths   5.06
5. three and four-tenths   3.4
6. eighty-six-hundredths   .86
7. twelve and four-hundredths   12.04
8. eight-hundredths   .08
9. ten and ten-tenths   10.10
10. fourteen-hundredths   .14
11. sixty-four-hundredths   .64
12. nine-tenths   .9

Study the examples below. Then, write each decimal in words in the space provided.

Examples:
4.8 = **four and eight-tenths**   3.45 = **three and forty-five-hundredths**

13. 3.25   three and twenty-five-hundredths
14. 5.2   five and two-tenths
15. .2   two-tenths
16. 95.26   ninety-five and twenty-six-hundredths
17. 2.2   two and two-tenths
18. .89   eight-nine-hundredths
19. 1.01   one and one-hundredths
20. .25   twenty-five-hundredths
21. .16   sixteen-hundredths
22. 25.12   twenty-five and twelve-hundredths
23. 14.1   fourteen and one-tenth
24. .55   fifty-five-hundredths
25. .69   sixty-nine-hundredths
26. 7.8   seven and eight-tenths
27. 3.0   three

Total Problems: Total Correct: Score: 55

© Carson-Dellosa CD-2211

Worksheet 56 — Adding and Subtracting Decimals

Name _____   Adding and Subtracting Decimals

Study the examples below. Add or subtract each problem and write the answer in the space provided. Rewrite any horizontal problem as a vertical problem, lining up the decimals.

Examples:

8.6 + 1.42 =

$\begin{array}{r} 8.60 \\ + 1.42 \\ \hline 10.02 \end{array}$ Add a 0 to fill in the empty space. Line up the decimal

3.1 − 2.18 =

$\begin{array}{r} 3.10 \\ - 2.18 \\ \hline 0.92 \end{array}$ Add a 0 to fill in the empty space. Line up the decimal points.

1. 6.4 + 9.3 =   15.7
2. $\begin{array}{r} 2.83 \\ + 1.39 \\ \hline 4.22 \end{array}$
3. 3.7 − 2.8 =   0.9
4. $\begin{array}{r} 43.8 \\ + 9.4 \\ \hline 53.2 \end{array}$
5. $\begin{array}{r} 5.9 \\ - 4.4 \\ \hline 1.5 \end{array}$
6. 4.68 + 6.7 =   11.38
7. $\begin{array}{r} 5.3 \\ - 2.1 \\ \hline 3.2 \end{array}$
8. 1.2 + 0.3 =   1.5
9. 95.6 − 82.12 =   13.48
10. $\begin{array}{r} 0.36 \\ + 0.87 \\ \hline 1.23 \end{array}$
11. 8.68 − 3.7 =   4.98
12. $\begin{array}{r} 0.52 \\ + 0.37 \\ \hline 0.89 \end{array}$
13. $\begin{array}{r} 4.24 \\ + 2.95 \\ \hline 7.19 \end{array}$
14. 6.8 − 2.5 =   4.3
15. $\begin{array}{r} 2.7 \\ + 8.9 \\ \hline 11.6 \end{array}$
16. 9.92 − 7.1 =   2.82
17. 43.8 + 14.12 =   57.92
18. $\begin{array}{r} 4.8 \\ - 3.7 \\ \hline 1.1 \end{array}$
19. 3.45 + 6.49 =   9.94
20. $\begin{array}{r} 16.10 \\ - 13.05 \\ \hline 3.05 \end{array}$

56   Total Problems: Total Correct: Score: © Carson-Dellosa CD-2211

Worksheet 57 — Multiplying Decimals

Name _____   Multiplying Decimals

Study the box below. Multiply each problem and write the answer in the space provided. Be sure to include a decimal point in the answer.

Rule:
1. Multiply as you would with whole numbers.
2. Count the number of digits to the right of the decimal point.
3. The product should have the same number of digits to the right of the decimal point.

Example:

$$\begin{array}{r} 3.7 \\ \times\ 6 \\ \hline 222 \end{array}$$

Multiply, then count the number of digits to the right of the decimal point.

$$\begin{array}{r} 3.7 \\ \times\ 6 \\ \hline 22.2 \end{array}$$

1. 2.8 × 6 = 16.8
2. 3.09 × 5 = 15.45
3. 8.3 × 4 = 33.2
4. 6.25 × 3 = 18.75
5. 97.44 × 7 = 682.08
6. 6.2 × 8 = 49.6
7. 5.14 × 8 = 41.12
8. 5.3 × 6 = 31.8
9. 79.9 × 6 = 479.4
10. 8.7 × 8 = 69.6
11. 14.3 × 6 = 85.8
12. 53 × .4 = 21.2
13. 139 × .6 = 83.4
14. 124 × .8 = 99.2
15. 49.5 × 4 = 198
16. 7.65 × 3 = 22.95
17. 3.8 × 5 = 19
18. 9.98 × 8 = 79.84
19. 10.5 × 5 = 52.5
20. 162 × .9 = 145.8

Total Problems: _____ Total Correct: _____ Score: _____   **57**

© Carson-Dellosa CD-2211

Worksheet 58 — Decimal Problem Solving

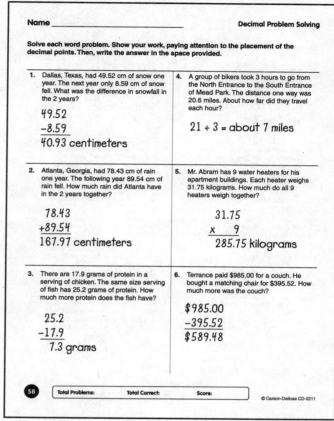

Name _____   Decimal Problem Solving

Solve each word problem. Show your work, paying attention to the placement of the decimal points. Then, write the answer in the space provided.

1. Dallas, Texas, had 49.52 cm of snow one year. The next year only 8.59 cm of snow fell. What was the difference in snowfall in the 2 years?

   49.52 − 8.59 = **40.93 centimeters**

2. Atlanta, Georgia, had 78.43 cm of rain one year. The following year 89.54 cm of rain fell. How much rain did Atlanta have in the 2 years together?

   78.43 + 89.54 = **167.97 centimeters**

3. There are 17.9 grams of protein in a serving of chicken. The same size serving of fish has 25.2 grams of protein. How much more protein does the fish have?

   25.2 − 17.9 = **7.3 grams**

4. A group of bikers took 3 hours to go from the North Entrance to the South Entrance of Mead Park. The distance one way was 20.6 miles. About how far did they travel each hour?

   21 ÷ 3 = **about 7 miles**

5. Mr. Abram has 9 water heaters for his apartment buildings. Each heater weighs 31.75 kilograms. How much do all 9 heaters weigh together?

   31.75 × 9 = **285.75 kilograms**

6. Terrance paid $985.00 for a couch. He bought a matching chair for $395.52. How much more was the couch?

   $985.00 − $395.52 = **$589.48**

58   Total Problems: _____ Total Correct: _____ Score: _____

© Carson-Dellosa CD-2211

Worksheet 59 — Elapsed Time

Name _____   Elapsed Time

Find each time. All times for problems 1–6 are P.M. Write the answer on the line provided.

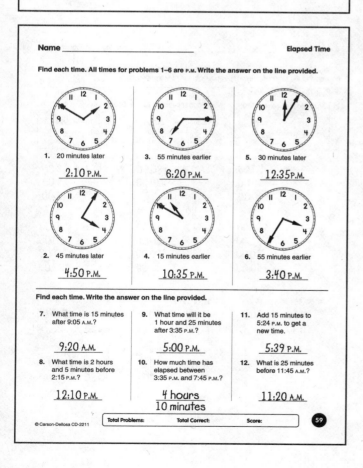

1. 20 minutes later — 2:10 P.M.
2. 45 minutes later — 4:50 P.M.
3. 55 minutes earlier — 6:20 P.M.
4. 15 minutes earlier — 10:35 P.M.
5. 30 minutes later — 12:35 P.M.
6. 55 minutes earlier — 3:40 P.M.

Find each time. Write the answer on the line provided.

7. What time is 15 minutes after 9:05 A.M.? — 9:20 A.M.
8. What time is 2 hours and 5 minutes before 2:15 P.M.? — 12:10 P.M.
9. What time will it be 1 hour and 25 minutes after 3:35 P.M.? — 5:00 P.M.
10. How much time has elapsed between 3:35 P.M. and 7:45 P.M.? — 4 hours 10 minutes
11. Add 15 minutes to 5:24 P.M. to get a new time. — 5:39 P.M.
12. What is 25 minutes before 11:45 A.M.? — 11:20 A.M.

© Carson-Dellosa CD-2211   Total Problems: _____ Total Correct: _____ Score: _____   **59**

Worksheet 60 — Reading a Calendar

Name _____   Reading a Calendar

Use the calendar to answer the following questions. Then, write the answer on the line provided.

| January |
Sunday	Monday	Tuesday	Wednesday	Thursday	Friday	Saturday
		1	2	3	4	5
6	7	8	9	10	11	12
13	14	15	16	17	18	19
20	21	22	23	24	25	26
27	28	29	30	31		

1. What day of the week is January 16? **Wednesday**
2. What is the date of the third Tuesday? **15**
3. How many Sundays are in the month? **4**
4. What day of the week is January 9? **Wednesday**
5. What day and date is exactly 9 days from the 15? **Thursday, 24**
6. What is the date of the first Friday? **4**
7. What day of the week will February 1 be? **Friday**
8. How many Saturdays are there in the month? **4**
9. What day of the week is January 29? **Tuesday**
10. On what date does the beginning of the third week fall? **13**

60   Total Problems: _____ Total Correct: _____ Score: _____

© Carson-Dellosa CD-2211

Worksheet 1 (61)

Name _____ Time Problem Solving

Solve each word problem. Show your work and write the answer in the space provided.

1. Mark left his house at 8:15 A.M. He was at work for 9 hours and 45 minutes. At what time did he return?

8:15 + 9 hours and 45 minutes = 6 P.M.

2. Meg started her workout session at 5:30 P.M. It lasted 65 minutes. What time did she finish?

5:30 + 1 hour + 5 minutes = 6:35 P.M.

3. Mr. Walters rode the bus to the stadium at 4:25 P.M. He returned that night at 11:35 P.M. How long was he gone?

11:35 − 4:25 = 7 hours 10 minutes

4. Chandra planned a business trip every Tuesday for an entire month. There were 30 days in the month, and her first trip was on the third. How many trips did she make that month?

4 trips

5. Reggie went to bed at 9:30 P.M. If he slept for 8 hours, when did he wake up the next morning?

9:30 + 8 hours = 5:30 A.M.

6. Monica wants to go to the ball game and to the movies. The ball game begins at 2:15 P.M. and lasts for 3 hours. The movie is at 5:00 P.M. Will she be able to attend both events the same day?

2:15 + 3 hours = 5:15

no

7. Sally began playing golf at 9:15 A.M. She played for 3 hours and took a break. She resumed playing at 2:00 P.M. and played until 5:00 that evening. How many hours in all did she play golf?

3 + 3 = 6 hours

8. Mrs. Jackson sends a postcard to her grandson every month on the 15th. If she does this for a full year, how many postcards will he receive in all?

12 x 1 = 12 postcards

Total Problems: _____ Total Correct: _____ Score: _____

© Carson-Dellosa CD-2211

Worksheet 2 (62)

Name _____ Adding and Subtracting Money

Study the examples below. Complete each problem. Remember to line up the decimal points. Rewrite any horizontal problem vertically. Then, write the answer in the space provided.

Examples:

$14.38 − $6.32 =
$14.38
− 6.32
$ 8.06

$13.01 + $10.62 =
$13.01
+ 10.62
$23.63

1. $38.42 + $16.45 =
$54.87

2. $36.14 − $16.44 =
$19.70

3. $142.36
   − 16.49
   $125.87

4. $16.42
   + 3.76
   $20.18

5. $54.41 − $10.01 =
$44.40

6. $49.38 + $114.69 =
$164.07

7. $76.16
   − 20.98
   $55.18

8. $46.38
   − 14.72
   $31.66

9. $980.25 − $42.21 =
$938.04

10. $883.74 + $16.52 =
$900.26

11. $95.88
   + 29.71
   $125.59

12. $600.00
   − 217.15
   $382.85

Total Problems: _____ Total Correct: _____ Score: _____

© Carson-Dellosa CD-2211

Worksheet 3 (63)

Name _____ Multiplying and Dividing Money

Study the box below. Complete each problem. Be sure to place the numbers in the correct place value and watch the placement of the decimal point. Write the answer in the space provided.

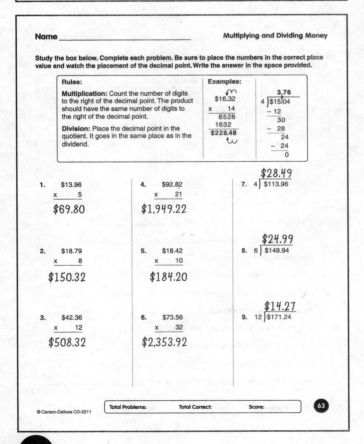

Rules:

Multiplication: Count the number of digits to the right of the decimal point. The product should have the same number of digits to the right of the decimal point.

Division: Place the decimal point in the quotient. It goes in the same place as in the dividend.

Examples:

$16.32
x   14
6528
1632
$228.48

3.76
4)$15.04
− 12
30
− 28
24
− 24
0

1. $13.96
   x   5
   $69.80

2. $18.79
   x   8
   $150.32

3. $42.36
   x   12
   $508.32

4. $92.82
   x   21
   $1,949.22

5. $18.42
   x   10
   $184.20

6. $73.56
   x   32
   $2,353.92

7. $28.49
4)$113.96

8. $24.99
6)$149.94

9. $14.27
12)$171.24

Total Problems: _____ Total Correct: _____ Score: _____

© Carson-Dellosa CD-2211

Worksheet 4 (64)

Name _____ Estimating Amounts of Money

Study the examples below. Estimate the sums and differences of money. Write the dollar sign and the decimal point in the answer in the space provided.

Examples:

Round to the nearest $0.10:
$0.85 → $0.90
+ 0.29 → + 0.30
$1.20

Round to the nearest $1.00:
$8.39 → $8.00
− 2.75 → − 3.00
$5.00

Round to the nearest $10.00:
$34.60 → $30.00
+ 47.30 → + 50.00
$80.00

1. $24.98 $20.00
   + 83.75   + 80.00
   $100.00

2. $49.64 $50.00
     26.05   30.00
   + 73.02 + 70.00
   $150.00

3. $0.46 + $0.43 + $0.27 =
$0.50 + $0.40 + $0.30 = $1.20

4. $0.53 + $0.28 =
$0.50 + 0.30 = $0.80

5. $26.75 $30.00
   − 19.83   − 20.00
   $10.00

6. $38.74 $40.00
     29.07   30.00
   + 56.86 + 60.00
   $130.00

7. $9.45 − $1.63 =
$9.00 − $2.00 = $7.00

8. $6.59 + $8.25 + $1.45 =
$7.00 + $8.00 + $1.00 = $16.00

9. $7.74 $ 8.00
   − 5.46   − 5.00
   $ 3.00

10. $18.25 $20.00
     14.45   10.00
   + 6.56 + 7.00
   $37.00

11. $45.78 − $26.09 =
$50.00 − $30.00 = $20.00

12. $0.56 − $0.33 =
$0.60 − $0.30 = $0.30

Total Problems: _____ Total Correct: _____ Score: _____

© Carson-Dellosa CD-2211

Page 65 — Money Problem Solving

Name _____

Money Problem Solving

Solve each word problem. Show your work and write the dollar sign and the decimal point in each answer in the space provided.

1. Kathleen had $15.00 to spend at the fair. She bought a hot dog and soda for $4.20. Kathleen spent $6.25 on a souvenir. How much money does Kathleen have after her purchases?

$4.20
+6.25
$10.45

$15.00
−10.45
$4.55

4. John spent $4.75 on food at the baseball game. He spent $13.27 on a souvenir hat. How much more did he spend on the food than on the hat?

$13.27
− 4.75
$8.52

2. Glen went to the store to buy items for his birthday party. He spent $14.23 on balloons and $28.32 for food. How much did Glen spend in all?

$14.23
+28.32
$42.55

5. Lisa earned $31.36 each week for delivering newspapers. She delivered newspapers for 2 weeks. How much money did Lisa earn after 2 weeks?

$31.36
x   2
$62.72

3. Last year, Jimmy earned $413.29 by selling his prize-winning carrot cake at the Georgia State Fair. This year, he earned $592.56. How much more did Jimmy earn this year?

$592.56
−$413.29
$179.27

6. Brittani wants to buy 2 shirts that are on sale. Each shirt is on sale for $14.50 including tax. If Brittani has $30.00, how much change will she get after purchasing 2 shirts?

$14.50
x   2
$29.00

$30.00
−29.00
$1.00

© Carson-Dellosa CD-2211

Total Problems: _____ Total Correct: _____ Score: _____   **65**

Page 66 — Metric Length and Mass

Name _____

Metric Length and Mass

Study the rules below. Then, write the answer on the line provided.

Rules:	
Length	**Weight**
10 millimeters (mm) = 1 centimeter (cm)	1 gram (g) = 1,000 milligrams (mg)
100 cm = 1 meter (m)	1,000 g = 1 kilogram (kg)
1,000 m = 1 kilometer (km)	

1. 2 meters = **200** centimeters
3. 20 centimeters = **200** millimeters
2. 3,200 grams = **3.2** kilograms
4. 8 kilograms = **8,000** grams

Choose the appropriate unit of measurement. Circle the letter beside the correct answer.

5. weight of a gold bracelet
A. kilograms   C. millimeters
(B.) grams   D. kilometers

8. weight of a dump truck
(A.) kilograms   C. centimeters
B. grams   D. kilometers

6. length of a kitchen table
A. millimeters   C. grams
(B.) meters   D. kilograms

9. weight of an orange
A. millimeters   C. kilograms
(B.) grams   D. centimeters

7. length of a pencil
(A.) centimeters   C. grams
B. meters   D. kilograms

10. length of chalkboard
(A.) meters   C. centimeters
B. kilometers   D. millimeters

66   Total Problems: _____ Total Correct: _____ Score: _____

© Carson-Dellosa CD-2211

Page 67 — Customary Length and Mass

Name _____

Customary Length and Mass

Study the rules below. Choose the unit that makes the statement reasonable. Then, write the answer on the line provided.

Rules:	
Length	**Weight**
1 foot (ft) = 12 inches (in)	16 ounces (oz) = 1 pound (lb)
1 yard (yd) = 3 ft = 36 in	2,000 lb = 1 ton
1 mile (mi) = 1,760 yd = 5,280 ft	

1. The football field is 100 **yards** long.

2. A milk truck weighs 4 **tons** .

3. The teacher's desk is 30 **inches** high.

4. An apple weighs 8 **ounces** .

5. It is 45 **miles** from Millersville to Bakerstown. The drive takes about 1 hour.

6. Jennifer's new compact disk weighs 6 **ounces** .

7. The ceiling in our classroom is 3 **yards** high.

8. Mark's mother's new gold necklace weighs 2 **ounces** .

9. Susan's father is about 6 **feet** tall.

10. Kayla's grandfather weighs 185 **pounds** .

© Carson-Dellosa CD-2211

Total Problems: _____ Total Correct: _____ Score: _____   **67**

Page 68 — Customary Capacity

Name _____

Customary Capacity

Study the rules below. Choose the best unit of measurement. Circle the letter beside the correct answer.

Rules:	
2 cups = 1 pint (pt)	4 qt = 1 gallon (gal)
2 pt = 1 quart (qt)	16 cups = 1 gal

1. bowl of soup
(A.) cup   C. quart
B. pint   D. gallon

4. water in a bathtub
A. cup   C. quart
B. pint   (D.) gallon

2. glass of juice
(A.) cup   C. quart
B. pint   D. gallon

5. pitcher of water
A. cup   (C.) quart
B. pint   D. gallon

3. A filled baby pool
A. cup   C. quart
B. pint   (D.) gallon

6. motor oil
A. cup   (C.) quart
B. pint   D. gallon

Study the example below. Then, write the answer on the line provided.

Example:
8 pints = _____ cups
1 pint equals 2 cups.
8 x 2 = 16 ⟶ 8 pints = **16** cups

7. 5 quarts = **10** pints
11. 3 gallons = **24** pints
8. 4 cups = **2** pints
12. 2 pints = **4** cups
9. **2** gallons = 16 pints
13. 5 gallons = **20** quarts
10. **4** pints = 2 quarts
14. 3 quarts = **12** cups

68   Total Problems: _____ Total Correct: _____ Score: _____

© Carson-Dellosa CD-2211

Sheet 1 — Measurement Problem Solving

Name _____   Measurement Problem Solving

Solve each word problem. Show your work and write the answer in the space provided.

1. Sally Rose made 8 quarts of punch for the birthday party. How many cups was that?

$$8 \times 2 = 16$$
$$16 \times 2 = 32 \text{ cups}$$

2. Two boxes of gold weigh 4 pounds 8 ounces. Each pound costs $400.00. How much are the boxes worth?

$$400 \times 4 = 1,600$$
$$1,600 + 200 = \$1,800$$

3. Years ago, containers were used to measure milk. If 4 containers equaled 1 quart, how many quarts of milk was 184 containers?

$$184 \div 4 = 46 \text{ quarts}$$

4. Mrs. Lackey wanted to give each child in her room a calculator. Each calculator weighed 16 ounces. If Mrs. Lackey gave each of her 20 students a calculator, how many pounds did the calculators weigh in all?

$$20 \times 1 = 20 \text{ pounds}$$

5. Virginia's school ordered 20 boxes of milk. In each box there were 35 containers of milk. On the last day, 265 containers were used. How many were left over?

$$35 \times 20 = 6,700$$
$$6,700 - 265 = 435 \text{ containers}$$

6. If a chef uses 10 cups of whole wheat flour for each 12 cups of white enriched flour, how many cups of white enriched flour are needed to go with 30 cups of whole wheat flour?

$$30 \div 10 = 3$$
$$12 \times 3 = 36 \text{ cups}$$

Total Problems: _____ Total Correct: _____ Score: _____ **69**

© Carson-Dellosa CD-2211

Sheet 2 — Polygons

Name _____   Polygons

Study the box below. Name each polygon. Tell how many sides and vertices there are. Write the answers on the lines provided.

Rule:
A **polygon** is a closed plane figure with 3 or more sides. A closed figure is a figure that has no open line segments. You can trace a line around the perimeter of a closed figure without ever coming to an end. The **vertex** is the point where 2 sides meet. More than 1 vertex is called **vertices**.

Example:
This is a quadrilateral with 4 sides and 4 vertices.

1. _6_ sides _6_ vertices
4. _3_ sides _3_ vertices
7. _8_ sides _8_ vertices
2. _4_ sides _4_ vertices
5. _4_ sides _4_ vertices
8. _4_ sides _4_ vertices
3. _4_ sides _4_ vertices
6. _3_ sides _3_ vertices
9. _5_ sides _5_ vertices

70 Total Problems: _____ Total Correct: _____ Score: _____

© Carson-Dellosa CD-2211

Sheet 3 — Symmetry

Name _____   Symmetry

Study the box below. Draw the line of symmetry on the following figures.

Rule:
A figure has a line of symmetry if it can be folded so that the two parts fit exactly (congruent).

Example:

answers may vary

1.
2.
3.
4.

Does the dashed line in each figure represent the line of symmetry? Check each answer yes or no.

5. _____ yes _✓_ no
6. _✓_ yes _____ no
7. _✓_ yes _____ no
8. _____ yes _✓_ no
9. _____ yes _✓_ no
10. _____ yes _✓_ no

© Carson-Dellosa CD-2211 Total Problems: _____ Total Correct: _____ Score: _____ **71**

Sheet 4 — Congruent Figures

Name _____   Congruent Figures

Study the box below. Decide if each pair is congruent. Then, circle the correct answer.

Rule:
When figures are the exact same size and shape, they are labeled congruent.

Example:
Congruent / Not Congruent

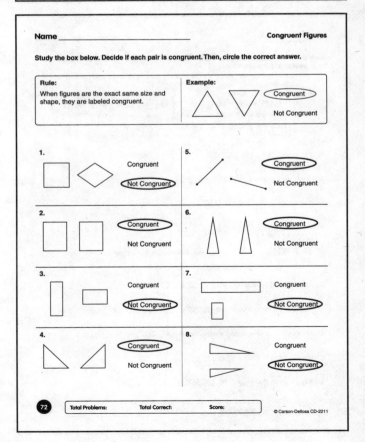

1. Congruent / (Not Congruent)
2. (Congruent) / Not Congruent
3. Congruent / (Not Congruent)
4. (Congruent) / Not Congruent
5. (Congruent) / Not Congruent
6. (Congruent) / Not Congruent
7. Congruent / (Not Congruent)
8. Congruent / (Not Congruent)

72 Total Problems: _____ Total Correct: _____ Score: _____

© Carson-Dellosa CD-2211

© Carson-Dellosa CD-2211

Worksheet 1 (top left)

Name _____   Lines, Line Segments, and Rays

Study the examples below. Identify each figure as a line, line segment, or ray. Be sure to label the figures with the correct symbols. Write the answer on the line provided.

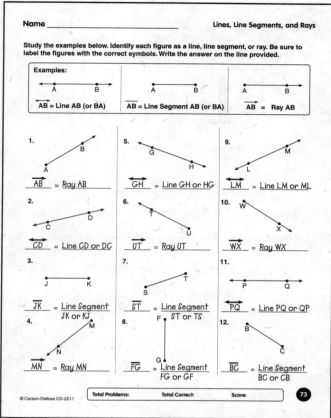

Examples:

$\overleftrightarrow{AB}$ = Line AB (or BA) $\overline{AB}$ = Line Segment AB (or BA) $\overrightarrow{AB}$ = Ray AB

1. $\overrightarrow{AB}$ = Ray AB
2. $\overleftrightarrow{CD}$ = Line CD or DC
3. $\overline{JK}$ = Line Segment JK or KJ
4. $\overrightarrow{MN}$ = Ray MN
5. $\overleftrightarrow{GH}$ = Line GH or HG
6. $\overrightarrow{UT}$ = Ray UT
7. $\overline{ST}$ = Line Segment ST or TS
8. $\overline{FG}$ = Line Segment FG or GF
9. $\overleftrightarrow{LM}$ = Line LM or ML
10. $\overrightarrow{WX}$ = Ray WX
11. $\overleftrightarrow{PQ}$ = Line PQ or QP
12. $\overline{BC}$ = Line Segment BC or CB

© Carson-Dellosa CD-2211   Total Problems: ___ Total Correct: ___ Score: ___ 73

Worksheet 2 (top right)

Name _____   Angles

Study the examples below. Identify each angle as a right angle, straight angle, acute angle, or obtuse angle. Write the answer on the line provided.

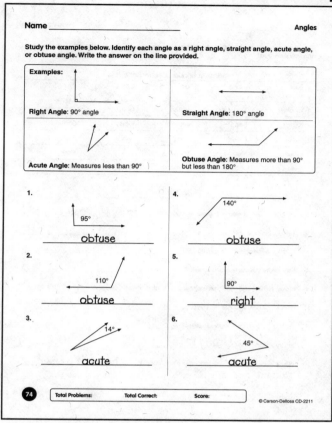

Examples:

Right Angle: 90° angle   **Straight Angle:** 180° angle

Acute Angle: Measures less than 90°   **Obtuse Angle:** Measures more than 90° but less than 180°

1. 95° obtuse
2. 110° obtuse
3. 14° acute
4. 140° obtuse
5. 90° right
6. 45° acute

74 Total Problems: ___ Total Correct: ___ Score: ___ © Carson-Dellosa CD-2211

Worksheet 3 (bottom left)

Name _____   Perimeter

Study the box below. Find the perimeter of each figure. Then, write the answer in the space provided.

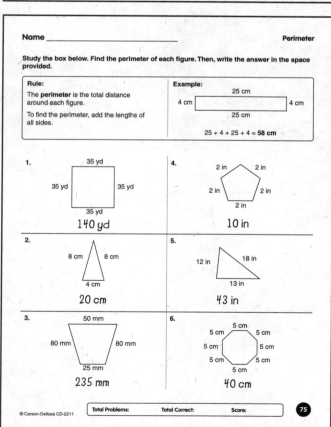

Rule:
The **perimeter** is the total distance around each figure.
To find the perimeter, add the lengths of all sides.

Example:
25 cm, 4 cm, 25 cm, 4 cm
25 + 4 + 25 + 4 = **58 cm**

1. 35 yd square 140 yd
2. 8 cm, 8 cm, 4 cm 20 cm
3. 50 mm, 80 mm, 80 mm, 25 mm 235 mm
4. 2 in pentagon 10 in
5. 12 in, 18 in, 13 in 43 in
6. 5 cm octagon 40 cm

© Carson-Dellosa CD-2211   Total Problems: ___ Total Correct: ___ Score: ___ 75

Worksheet 4 (bottom right)

Name _____   Area

Study the box below. Find the area of each figure. Write the answer on the line provided.

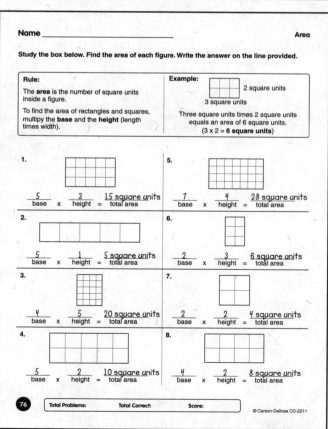

Rule:
The **area** is the number of square units inside a figure.
To find the area of rectangles and squares, multiply the **base** and the **height** (length times width).

Example: 2 square units, 3 square units
Three square units times 2 square units equals an area of 6 square units.
(3 x 2 = **6 square units**)

1. $\dfrac{5}{\text{base}}$ x $\dfrac{3}{\text{height}}$ = 15 square units (total area)
2. $\dfrac{5}{\text{base}}$ x $\dfrac{1}{\text{height}}$ = 5 square units (total area)
3. $\dfrac{4}{\text{base}}$ x $\dfrac{5}{\text{height}}$ = 20 square units (total area)
4. $\dfrac{5}{\text{base}}$ x $\dfrac{2}{\text{height}}$ = 10 square units (total area)
5. $\dfrac{7}{\text{base}}$ x $\dfrac{4}{\text{height}}$ = 28 square units (total area)
6. $\dfrac{2}{\text{base}}$ x $\dfrac{3}{\text{height}}$ = 6 square units (total area)
7. $\dfrac{2}{\text{base}}$ x $\dfrac{2}{\text{height}}$ = 4 square units (total area)
8. $\dfrac{4}{\text{base}}$ x $\dfrac{2}{\text{height}}$ = 8 square units (total area)

76 Total Problems: ___ Total Correct: ___ Score: ___ © Carson-Dellosa CD-2211

© Carson-Dellosa CD-2211

Answer Key

Name _____ Reading a Table

Study the table below. Use the information to answer each question. Write the answer on the line provided.

Student Music Lesson Schedule

DAY 1 (new students only)	DAY 2	DAY 3	DAY 4	DAY 5
Nicole	José	Solina	Greg	Jamie
Naomi	Kira	Jamie	Kipley	Solina
Tanya	Kipley	Greg	Jacob	Rebecca
Michelle	Mark	Rebecca	José	Mark
Fiora	Jacob	Margaret	Kira	Drake

1. When does Nicole have her music lesson? Day 1
2. Other than Jacob, who has a lesson on day 4? Greg, Kipley, José, & Kira
3. Tanya, Naomi, and Fiora all have a lesson on which day? Day 1
4. When is Drake's lesson? Day 5
5. How many lessons is Jacob scheduled for in all? 2
6. Kipley, Naomi, and Mark practice together. Who is the new music student? Naomi
7. How many new students are there? 5
8. What days does Jamie have lessons? 3, 5
9. When is Fiora's lesson? Day 1
10. Why do you think Mark does not have a lesson on day 1? he is not a new student

© Carson-Dellosa CD-2211   Total Problems: ___ Total Correct: ___ Score: ___   77

Name _____ Reading Graphs

Study the bar graph below. Use the information to answer each question on the line provided.

Subjects Students Like

Key: 3rd Grade (white), 4th Grade (black)

1. Which grade level liked math better? fourth grade
2. Which subject did both grade levels like equally? science
3. Which grade level liked reading better? 4
4. What is the most popular subject in these grades? math

Study the pictograph below. Use the information to answer each question on the line provided.

Tires Sold

Month	Number of Tires Sold
Jan.	○○○○○⌒
Feb.	○○
March	○⌒
April	○○○⌒
May	○

Key: ○ = 500 tires

5. How many more tires were sold in April than in February? 750
6. What is the difference between the least number of tires sold and the greatest number of tires sold? 2,250

78   Total Problems: ___ Total Correct: ___ Score: ___   © Carson-Dellosa CD-2211

96

© Carson-Dellosa CD-2211